LEADING CHRISTIANS TO CHRIST

Evangelizing the Church

Rob Smith

MOREHOUSE PUBLISHING
Harrisburg, PA • Wilton, CT

Morehouse Publishing

Editorial office
78 Danbury Road
Wilton, CT 06897

Corporate office
P.O. Box 1321
Harrisburg, PA 17105

Library of Congress Cataloging-in-Publication Data

Smith, Rob.
    Leading Christians to Christ: evangelizing the church/Rob Smith.
      p. cm.
    Includes bibliographical references.
    ISBN 0-8192-1529-5
    1. Evangelistic work—Philosophy. 2. Church renewal—Episcopal Church.
3. Episcopal Church—Membership. 4. Episcopal Church—Doctrines.
5. Anglican Communion—Membership. 6. Anglican Communion—Doctrines.
I. Title.
BX5969.S55   1990
269'.2—dc20   90-31634
                                                     CIP

Printed in the United States of America
by
BSC LITHO
Harrisburg, PA 17105

*To Adrian Caceres and Luis Caisapanta,
bishops extraordinary,
and to the priests and people of the
Iglesia Episcopal del Ecuador
where the Church is being liberated
and los pobres won for Christ.*

The Cover: The cover design includes the logo of the new episcopal mission being established by Father Rob Smith in Coppell, Texas. The mission, The Church of the Apostles (Episcopal), is being started on the basis of church growth principles. The Jerusalem cross, the logo for "The Apostles" has been interpreted by some as representing the wounds of Christ, by others as Christ in the midst of the Gospel evangelists, and by the new mission as representing one church that emphasized the Apostles' teaching, the fellowship, the breaking of bread and the prayers marking the nature of the early church in Acts 2:42.

ACKNOWLEDGMENTS

I owe a serious debt of gratitude to my wife Diana who as an accomplished lay theologian has always insisted that I keep my feet on the ground and my theology connected to life. During the writing of this she worked outside of the home and I stayed at home with my son Timothy and my daughter Juliana. Timothy had an unwavering confidence in the eventual publication of this manuscript which he demonstrated by dragging his friends over to the computer corner in the dining room to see "the book my dad is writing." Juliana gave those gentle graceful infusions of love-at-the-right-moment that provide the fuel for nurturing parents as they go about their labors.

I owe a debt of gratitude to my educators, notably to Edward Rochie Hardy, a brilliant man who could be unusually humble. His advice to read two ancient classics of theology for every contemporary book, provided the spark that rounded out my education after leaving seminary. Notable among my other educators is the laity of the congregations in which I have served for the past twenty years. Their struggles with the issues of the gospel have provided some of the impetus for the development of my understanding of evangelism within the Church.

I owe a debt of gratitude to a very special friend, Cordelia Koplow. Her combination of theological acumen and sensitive feel for grammar and clarity in writing were invaluable in the preparation of the original manuscript. From this one work she has collected an entire bushel basket of commas that I will be able to use at a later date, preferably in a more sparing fashion. It was Cordelia who not only tended the manuscript from chapter to chapter as it was produced, but also brought to my attention several valuable sources.

Rob Smith
Coppell, Texas
Spring 1990

You, Christ, are the king of glory
the eternal Son of the Father.
When you became man to set us free
you did not shun the Virgin's womb.
You overcame the sting of death
and opened the kingdom of heaven to all believers.
You are seated at God's right hand in glory.
We believe that you will come and be our judge.
Come then, Lord, and help your people,
bought with the price of your own blood,
and bring us with your saints
to glory everlasting.

— —Te Deum Laudamus, fourth century A.D.
The Book of Common Prayer

Contents

Introduction

One of the most difficult tasks before clergy in the Episcopal Church is the evangelization of nominal Christians within existing parishes. The difficulty presents itself on several levels and presents Episcopal clergy with some serious practical and theological problems.

The Sunday morning congregation includes people of all levels of theological understanding and faith, from the apparently barely conscious worshiper who seems to be fulfilling some vaguely perceived obligation to be there to the radical enthusiast of "being there" who may or may not have any desire to be touched on deeper levels. In every congregation, some are consciously children of God, some would like to be, and a number of people have deep fears about reaching for a personal relationship with God. To this last group, challenge to faith is a strong irritant, and that is especially true when the invitation is couched in evangelical jargon. In contrast, we have the stark claim of the late Anglican evangelist David Watson, who said, "Man is not the slightest use to God, until he is converted and knows it."[1]

The Episcopal Church, as many Episcopalians are fond of noting, is a bridge church that stands in a balance between the Roman Catholic Church and a variety of Protestant denominations. As such, the Episcopal Church is host to a wide variety of people who come through its doors drawn by its ambience. Most Episcopalians love its liturgy, the centrality of the eucharist, its *Book of Common Prayer*, and its traditions. Such things as vestments, candles, altars, music, stained-glass saints, needlepoint cushions, kneeling, standing, bowing, in some places genuflecting, congregational participation in written prayers, and a myriad of other small touches appeal to the sensibilities of those who elect to come and be part of the Episcopal Church. Worshipers who are comfortable juggling a Sunday morning bulletin, a prayer book, a hymnal, books of alternative service music, and perhaps a pew Bible are, in general, going to be fairly well educated and able to tolerate the small library of sources found in the average pew of a local Episcopal parish. An informal poll of the adults in any Episcopal congregation will instantly reveal that the cradle Episcopalians are generally out-numbered by those who have come from other denominations. One result of this is that those who have elected to become Episcopalians have not been drawn generally by evangelistic methodologies but by the ambience of the Episcopal Church. This ambience has its validity as an evangelistic tool. For many, the presence of God is mediated by beauty, drama, and orderliness, but the ambience can also be a shield against the encroachment of the presence of God.

Episcopal clergy have to thread their way through a wide variety of resistances to the proclamation of a gospel that calls people to a personal faith. While on the one hand there is a temptation to abandon the traditions and the ambience in order to make the message clear, there is, on the other hand, a set of theological issues that must be dealt with for clergy and laity alike in the process of calling people to a personal faith. The mere assertion that a personal faith is necessary and that Episcopalians need to be converted is apt to be hotly debated by Episcopalians. Objections range from concerns over the meaning and efficacy of baptism and its relation to confirmation down to the remark of one of my parishioners who years ago retorted, "I live a good life. I'll get there!" There is an unresolved debate in Anglican circles over the nature of baptism, how baptismal grace works and what it means, and what is the relation of confirmation to baptism. Of this debate, the Church Teaching Series says, "It seems fair to say that this divergence of viewpoint lies deep within Anglican thought. No definitive resolution has appeared, and no easy answers are available."[2] In the light of that reality, how are we to understand the call to conversion and personal faith as a mandate for the Church today? How do we understand conversion in a context where many people, by virtue of frequent repetition of creedal statements, have no obvious difficulty with giving intellectual assent to the doctrines of faith? How do we understand conversion in the midst of congregations where to all intents and purposes the people we seek to convert are already incorporated into the visible Body of Christ?

The centrality of Jesus also becomes an issue. In my first parish, an elderly Episcopalian stated her objection to me with remarkable clarity when she said, "Young man, you not only talk too much about Jesus, but you also make the mistake of praying to him." What rightful place does the call to a personal relationship with Jesus have within the context of the Episcopal Church?

The answer to these questions makes up a necessary part of the background to an approach to the evangelization of nominal Christians within Episcopal congregations. The key to the process of evangelism and the call to conversion, and a personalized faith, is not for the Episcopalian in the negation of the tradition and ambience of the Episcopal Church but in a wise use of the structure that already exists. Baptism and confirmation in the Episcopal Church do not stand alone but as the pro-Anaphora (or service of "The Word of God") of the Holy Eucharist. Years ago I remember a Pentecostal pastor sitting in one of the pews of an Episcopal Church I was serving in. He was thumbing through *The Book of Common Prayer* with tears running down his cheeks and was overheard by one of my parishioners as he mumbled repeatedly, "It's all there. It's all there!" Baptism, confirmation, and Holy Eucharist combined with the teaching and pastoral care that accompanies them are powerful tools for evangelism.

To the extent that the call to conversion and a personalized faith is effective, it will call forth varying degrees of opposition. A brief glance at the Book of Acts will verify the historical validity of this. One of the major blocks in the evangelization of nominal Christians is a sense of fear and antipathy aroused by the nature of the gospel itself. An effective proclamation of the Kingdom of God invites the individual into an acceptance of personal reality in the light of the holiness and grace of God. Initially, few like to be called into account and told that surrender to grace is the only way to truly become part of the Church, especially when they have from the beginning made the assumption that they already belong. It is inescapable that the good news is bad news for some at its first hearing. But for many others the gospel is good news, and it is for them that Jesus came, as he said, "Those who are well have no need of a physician, but those who are sick; I came not to call the righteous, but sinners."[3]

Notes

1. David Watson, "Evangelism in the Local Church" (Class lecture at Fuller Theological Seminary, Pasadena, CA, January 4–15, 1982).

2. Charles P. Price and Louis Weil, *Liturgy for Living*, Church Teaching Series (Seabury Press: New York, 1979), 124–25.

3. Matt. 9:12 RSV.

1. Is Conversion Really Necessary?

A Look at Basic Presuppositions

Presuppositions underlie all theology. Knowing this simplifies any attempt to understand why people support or oppose any theological assertion. From my point of view four presuppositions have a direct bearing on the question "Is conversion really necessary?" The presuppositions are paired with a negative and a positive side: God is, or he is not. God communicates, or he does not communicate. Jesus is the self-communication of God, or he is not. Miracles happen, or they do not. These presuppositions are not susceptible to proof. They are, however, often held with tremendous emotional force because they spring from the very core of each individual's response to reality. O.C. Edwards quite correctly warns us that

> our beliefs about God are our ultimately most inclusive categories for the interpretation of our experience. Now all of our categories are susceptible to modification. Piaget has pointed out that the mind is constantly at work, not only assimilating our sensations to the categories we already have, but also in accommodating those categories so that they are more adequate to the variety of sensations we experience. Since, however, we depend on those categories for being able to cope with the flood of sensations we experience, those categories need to be as stable as possible, so the mind has a great resistance to the necessity of accommodation. It only changes its categories when it is forced to do so. The more inclusive the category, the more resistant it is to change. Thus our fundamental ideas about the universe, such as our beliefs about God, are changed only under necessity and never without a sense of great threat to the personality.[1]

The four presuppositions are interdependent. The first three are given in logical order. The last one directly relates to the first three presuppositions. We either believe that God is or that he is not. Great figures in theology and philosophy from Thomas Aquinas to Bertrand Russell have argued both sides of the question thoroughly enough to convince us that neither side can be proved. If we believe that God exists, we have to ask what we mean by God. If we will allow one attribute of God, that of omnipotence, all the rest will logically follow. From a logical standpoint, if we do not allow omnipotence we are talking of a god, rather than God. If God exists

1

in that sense it is apparent that he can communicate with us both individually and corporately. Whether he does is a matter of faith and experimentation. At issue, of course, is the question "Can God communicate either his displeasure or his love to us and to me as an individual?" If the answer is yes, and if we believe that this God is omnipotent, then there is no logical difficulty in believing that Jesus could be the self-communication of God. The answer to that is again a matter of faith and intensely personal mystical experimentation and perception. If we believe that God exists, that he can communicate disfavor or love, and that he communicates himself fully in Jesus, then there is ample ground for accepting the call to a personal encounter with God in Jesus Christ our Lord. If, on the other hand, our basic presuppositions bar the likelihood of these beliefs, then a challenge to our stance will threaten the very core of our being. The fourth presupposition relates directly to the first three. If we believe that God exists in the sense given above, then it is reasonable to believe that God can work miracles, that he can work miracles as part of his communication to me, that he will do so in relationship to his self-communication through Jesus his Son, and that I will be able to know these miracles in my own personal experience. If my basic presuppositions allow that, then the miracle of spiritual rebirth, or conversion, becomes a possibility as well as the lesser miracles of God's intervention in a myriad of ways ranging from answers to simple prayers to miracles of healing.

If our presuppositions do not support these evangelical conclusions, then a presentation of a gospel calling us to conversion and to a personal encounter with Jesus, and through him with the Father, can be very threatening. As O.C. Edwards has said, ". . . our fundamental ideas about the universe, such as our beliefs about God, are changed only under necessity and never without a sense of great threat to the personality."[2] When the proclamation of the gospel is accompanied by signs and wonders, a dimension is added that both adds enticement to the gospel and deepens the threat of the gospel in the experience of the hearer.

The Place of Holy Scripture

The establishment of a foundation for our understanding of conversion depends in part on how one regards Holy Scripture. If Holy Scripture is not conceived of as an adequate expression of the mind of God, it becomes very difficult to find a rational basis for theological expression. This, however, is the predicament of a great number of church members whose only familiarity with the Bible is the Sunday lectionary reading in Holy Eucharist.

O.C. Edwards, a past professor of New Testament and patristics at Nashota House and current professor of homiletics at Seabury-Western Theological Seminary, is a well-known figure in the Episcopal Church. In his address, "An Overview of Evangelism in the Church—New Testament Times to the Present," given at the Episcopal Conference on Evangelism in Dallas, Texas, in January 1976, Edwards gives a clear picture of both his view of Scripture and his view of contemporary evangelism.[3] He, in a lucid way, gives theological expression to the perceptions and fears of many Episcopalians who sit in the pews of average Episcopal parishes.

On the development of his attitude toward Holy Scripture, he says this of his childhood perceptions in a fundamentalist environment:

> Let me see if I can summarize what we all believed. Every word in the Bible is literally, historically true. The Bible tells of the omnipotent God who created the world and everything in it in a calendar week of seven twenty-four-hour days. The first man and woman that he made, Adam and Eve, disobeyed him and were cast from the bliss of the garden of Eden and all their descendants have suffered from their Fall.[4]

Although Edwards is representative of many who are drawn to the Episcopal Church from other denominations, his childhood perception of Holy Scripture is not very different from the naive perception of church school children in many Episcopal parishes. This view sets the individual up for unfortunate confrontations with science. Edwards says,

> I can still remember vividly when I accidentally opened a zoology textbook to the page on which was printed a chart showing the skeletons of the major groups of vertebrates. From that moment on I could not doubt evolution and I could not believe in the literal historicity of the early chapters of Genesis. And that was not all. The doctrine of inerrancy had made the authority of the Bible an all or nothing proposition. If you could not believe every word of it, what reliance could you put on any of it? Thus began an advance in skepticism that did not halt until at seminary I came under the influence of the then prevalent theological liberalism that saw no special place for Jesus in theology beyond being a religious genius, a great teacher and example.[5]

His resolution of the matter may not give adequate ground for working out a theology of evangelism, but his view is characteristic of many whom he has taught and others who have been taught by them. He says,

> Classical Christian orthodoxy does not depend on biblical literalism. We all became quite fond of saying with Reinhold Niebuhr that the myths of the Bible did not have to be taken literally, but they did have to be taken seriously. While Genesis does not teach us accurate astronomy, geology, or history, it does teach us religion that is a great deal more accurate and adequate than our pseudo-sophistication.[6]

While his solution is considerably more erudite than that of the average person in the pew, he nevertheless reflects an attitude that elevates theology over Holy Scripture and makes approach to evangelism among Episcopalians somewhat problematic. Added to that is a general ignorance of the Bible in many congregations. I remember several years ago the problem that arose when pew Bibles were introduced into the parish I was serving. After announcing a New Testament reading and its page number, I looked up at the page-shuffling congregation and realized that I also needed to add the information that the New Testament was in the back section of the Bible.

Bishop Charles Gore gives another viewpoint:

> And we caught the note of the same spirit in the early Church, especially under the influence of the Greek Fathers. They conceive of the doctrinal authority of the Church as a restricted thing— restricted by Scripture. . . . The Church says to the convert, You must accept the message as the word of God on Faith; but your faith should grow into understanding. It will make you intellectually as well as morally free.
>
> If this be the true method, it has two enemies. The first is the temper which treats all acceptance of truth on authority as degrading; and in particular appears to deprecate in religion the very idea of a divine word received in faith—a divine message such as can be expressed in true propositions and embodied in historic facts. It would apparently interpret intellectual liberty to mean that each man must start for himself to discover what he can about God and human destiny.[7]

Although Gore wrote this in the 1920s, he has underlined a problem that is still current in the Episcopal Church today. Episcopalians in general tend to look toward Holy Scripture, tradition, and reason, not necessarily in that order, as the basis for authority. It remains much easier for Episcopalians to see that tradition must be subjected to Holy Scripture than it is for us to see that reason also must be subjected to Holy Scripture. To the extent that reason is elevated above Holy Scripture we run the danger of having our theology dominated by our presuppositions. Karl Barth underscores the limits of reason:

> Even the smallest, strangest, simplest, or obscurest among the biblical witnesses has an incomparable advantage over even the most pious, scholarly, and sagacious latter-day theologian. From his special point of view and in his special fashion, the witness has thought, spoken, and written about the revelatory Word and act in direct confrontation with it. All subsequent theology, as well as the whole of the community that comes after the event, will never find itself in the same immediate confrontation. . . . If theology seeks to learn this or that important truth but one thing is necessary—and with respect to this one thing on which all else depends, the biblical witnesses are better informed than are the theologians. For this reason theology must agree to let *them* look over its shoulder and correct its notebooks.[8]

To develop a theology of evangelism, one must be willing to take Scripture on its own terms rather than filtering it through critical presuppositions. If not an acceptance of the message "as the word of God on Faith,"[9] then at least one must maintain an open-minded respect. "Reverence," as Goethe was fond of pointing out, "is the first quality requisite for learning."[10]

A Biblical View of Conversion

Certain words common in evangelical circles raise red flags in the minds of Episcopalians. Basic biblically oriented words and phrases, such as *born again, repent, hell, baptism in the Spirit,* and *conversion,* have been to some extent banalized by thoughtless presentations. The fact that these expressions convey, and sometimes cloak, life-shaking realities only deepens the difficulty of hearing the words in their biblical meaning rather than layered with our cultural presuppositions and fears. The word *conversion* needs to be translated for Episcopalians. It derives from the Latin root *conversio,* and it simply means turning from one thing to another.[11] In Holy Scripture the three concepts of "repentance, penitence, and conversion are closely linked."[12] The Old Testament Hebrew verb for "convert" is *shubh,* which in general means to "turn around," "return," "bring back," or "restore."[13] While it is one of the most common verbs in the Old Testament, it also occurs with "the specifically theological meaning c. 120 times: turn round, return, be converted, bring back, in the sense of a change in behavior and of a return to the living God."[14] The meanings "return" and "bring back" have specific and obvious applications to environments where by virtue of a sacramental act—either circumcision or a sacrament, baptism—one is believed to already have been incorporated into the family of God in one's infancy. From that perspective all of us need to be converted more than once. Nothing protects baptized church members from the criticism of the Lord through Jeremiah: "all the house of Israel is uncircumcised in heart."[15] When we note that baptism is the new convenant replacement for circumcision, the application becomes clear. In Col. 2:11, the New International Version adequately reflects the underlying meaning of the Greek:

> In him you were also circumcised, in the putting off of the sinful nature, not with a circumcision done by the hands of men but with the circumcision done by Christ, having been buried with him in baptism and raised with him through your faith in the power of God, who raised him from the dead.[16]

The Word of the Lord through Jeremiah can be directed to circumcised and baptized alike: "Return [*shubh*], faithless Israel." [17] The word in the New Testament that expresses the force of *shubh* is *metanoneo*.[18] The noun form, *metanoia*, occurs twenty-two times in the New Testament; the verb form thirty-four times. The basic meaning of *metanoia* is "change of mind," "repentance," and "conversion." [19] But "the predominantly intellectual understanding of *metanoia* as change of mind plays very little part in the [New Testament]. Rather the decision by the whole man to turn around is stressed."[20]

Even a cursory reading of the New Testament will reveal that the call to repentance, or turning around (i.e., conversion), is a dominant theme and is used in calling those who worship another god and those who have strayed from the true God to turn to God through Jesus Christ. The call to repent, to turn toward God, or to be converted is consistently heard from the proclamation of John the baptizer in Mark 1:4 to Jesus, who proclaimed the call to repentance or conversion in relationship to the manifestation of the kingdom in Mark 1:15, to the Book of Acts and the apostolic preaching as in Acts 2:38, and to letters to the churches in the revelation to John.

While the words *repentance* or *conversion* are not explicitly mentioned in some other accounts, the meaning is quite clear.

The story of Nicodemus coming to Jesus by night occurs in the Prayer Book in two of the three year cycles of Sunday eucharist readings: in lectionary A on the second Sunday in Lent; in lectionary B on Trinity Sunday; but not in lectionary C.[21] It also occurs in the alternate readings for various occasions, as an option for "At Baptism," where it can be used as an alternate to the usual Gospel appointed for that Sunday. As a result it has a chance of being heard by the majority of Episcopalians regular in worship at least once every three years, during the Lenten season when attendance is higher. Older Episcopalians are more familiar with the passage, as it occurred on Trinity Sunday every year. Nevertheless, most Episcopalians are probably more familiar with its central challenge from billboards, gospel stickers and tracts, and neon signs. The command "Ye must be born again" is generally heard with a variety of reactions from irritation to humor.[22] It is interesting to note that the Trinity Sunday reading for lectionary B stops one verse short of this awkward statement.

It is sometimes difficult to hear a text like this. In part its meaning for us lies in the knowledge that Nicodemus was an acknowledged teacher of Israel and a member of the ruling Sanhedrin. Even a man so firmly rooted within the covenants of Israel needed to hear that message. For Nicodemus there was a surprising freshness in the approach of Jesus. Stunned, he retorts, "How can a man be born when he is old? Can he enter a second time into his mother's womb and be born?"[23] Nicodemus is consciously a self-proclaimed child of the covenant and finds himself in the difficult position of being told that his inclusion in the kingdom does not depend on his heritage or the sacramental act of circumcision but on spiritual rebirth.

The call to new life extended to Nicodemus is essentially a call inviting a child of the covenant to return from the formalism of his religion to a religion of the heart. The parable of the prodigal son in Luke 15:11–32, addressing those who unlike Nicodemus have rejected the covenant, emphasizes the return to the Father of a child that has strayed. Despite the fact that the intended audience is different, the message is essentially the same. To enter the kingdom one must be converted.

Among other accounts featuring the conversion theme are the stories of Lydia and the Philippian jailer in Acts 16:11–40. The former is the story of a Jewish proselyte, whose process of conversion had already begun, quietly opening her heart and asking to be baptized.[24] The second is the story of the stormy conversion of a worshiper of other gods on the verge of suicide receiving through Paul a completely new orientation and understanding. While the words *repent* or *conversion* are not used in any of the above stories, the concept is quite clear.

Conversion from the Perspective
of the Episcopal Renewal Movement

One of the foremost advocates of renewal in the Episcopal Church is Everett L. Fullam. Fullam is insistent about the personal nature of our faith. He says, ". . . if our religion is to be accepted by Almighty God, it must be a religion of the heart, and no outward performance."[25] He directly takes to task our tendency toward formalism:

> Do you see then, in all our ecclesiastical traditions, there are trees that are not of God's planting? Are we to expect that ritual and ceremony, as a replacement for worship that rises out of the depths of our beings, represents an acceptable substitute in the sight of the holy God? I think not.[26]

Fullam's point is clear and generally valid, but it seems to place ritual and ceremony in an exclusively negative position and theoretical, heartfelt spontaneity in the opposite positive role. Ritual and ceremony can be either blocks to true worship or, correctly taken, glorious vehicles of it. On the other hand, spontaneity without form evaporates very quickly into repetition and custom and, unless thought through very carefully, results in an inferior ritual and ceremony that is even less valid than the one that has been abandoned. This tendency for an overstated critique, always a temptation of new reformations, makes it more difficult for the thoughtful listener to hear the main point. The main point is simply that whether we use simple or elaborate ritual and ceremony, whether we treasure spontaneity or order, our worship is not valid unless it is a worship that flows out from the very center of our beings.

Fullam states with clarity one of the strongest emphases of renewal movements today, that of the centrality of Jesus Christ for the Christian. He says, "The essence of the Christian faith is not found in the teachings of Jesus, as important as those are, but rather in the Person of Jesus."[27] And again, "God's message to the human race, you see, is not a doctrine, an idea, a teaching, a principle, or a philosophy. It is a Person, a Word become flesh, and we know Him as Jesus Christ."[28] This has a direct bearing on worship: "So I believe that worship that is pleasing and acceptable in the sight of God is worship that centers in Jesus Christ and is in harmony with holy Scripture."[29] It is worth noting that Jesus accepted the worship of men both before and after the resurrection.[30]

Fullam's understanding of the biblical nature of conversion is very clear:

Conversion looms large in New Testament thought. To present Christ in such a way as to elicit faith in Him was the aim and purpose of apostolic preaching. The early Church was made up of people who had been changed by the power of God and went about everywhere proclaiming the transforming message of the Gospel.

They were themselves converted, transformed, changed. They spoke as converts. They knew something had happened to them. The entrance of Christ into their lives had made all things new.[31]

The conversion Fullam speaks of is not just a conversion to God. It is specifically a conversion to Jesus Christ, and Jesus Christ is the central content of that conversion. He quotes Archbishop William Temple in underlining the centrality of Jesus in this experience:

I am impressed by the definition of evangelism given by the great Anglican Archbishop of Canterbury, William Temple.

To evangelize, he said, is "so to present Christ Jesus in the power of the Holy Spirit that men shall come to put their trust in God through Him, to accept Him as their Savior, and to serve Him as their King in the fellowship of the Church."[32]

Temple in part echoes an older sentiment from an anonymous seventeenth-century devotional classic:

This is the Sum of that SECOND COVENANT we are now under, wherein you see what Christ hath done, how he Executes those Three Great Offices of KING, PRIEST and PROPHET: as also what is required of us, without our faithful performance of which, all that he hath done, shall never stand us in any stead; for he will never be a Priest to save any, who take him not as well for their Prophet to Teach, as their King to Rule them; nay, if we neglect our part of this Covenant, our condition will be yet worse than if it had never been made; for we shall then be to Answer, not for the breach of Law only, as in the first, but for the abuse of mercy, which is of all sins the most provoking.[33]

Whether one looks at the theme of conversion from the perspective of the contemporary renewal movement or from the perspective of its older antecedents, the message is the same. We have a responsibility not only to accept him as our priestly sacrifice but also as our teacher, and both of these responses are inseparable from relating to him in the present as our King. To neglect this last responsibility is to abuse mercy. Fullam drives the point home:

It may be that someone reading these words has been baptized, and even nurtured by the Church, but has never put personal faith in Jesus Christ. . . .

If you have not invited Jesus into your life, then according to the
New Testament you are a Christian in name only. . . .
Believing and being baptized are both part of what it means to
become a Christian. Our God is calling each one of us to become
a Christian in fact as well as in name.[34]

Predictably, this approach evokes strong reactions from other
Episcopalians, but they must also contend with the witness of the
church fathers. It was no less than Tertullian who said, "Men are
made, not born, Christians."[35]

Looking at a Major Negative Reaction

Before looking directly at O.C. Edwards' reaction to the type of
approach represented by Fullam, it is necessary to place Edwards
in the broader context of the Episcopal Church. Those outside our
denomination may not appreciate the benefits of Episcopalian
broad-mindedness and tolerance. There is no such thing as a pure
church, but every denomination is like a field with weeds in it.
Episcopalians may strongly disagree with each other but at the same
time would be very loath to venture the opinion that the other
person is a weed to be rooted out now or later. Edwards is a well-
respected professor of an Episcopal seminary and verbalizes one of
two major responses to the message of fellow Episcopalians. The
other major response is acceptance of the message and its implications for the transformation of life.

Edwards himself points to the breadth and vitality of the Anglican
Communion:

I think I am correct in remembering Archbishop Donald Arden
of South Africa to have said that the Anglican Church in Africa is
growing faster than anywhere else in the world and that there will
soon be more black than white Anglicans in the world. We need to
find ways to cooperate which will recognize our status as the junior
if more affluent partner.[36]

The Anglican Communion, of which the Episcopal Church is a
part, is a far-flung net, yet within there is a common sensibility.

Basic to the Standing Committee's decision . . . stands a theological
judgement about Anglicanism and its spirituality. . . . It is, expressed
simply, that God meets the needs of the Church and all its members
with their differing temperaments and cultures in different ways.
Moreover, Anglicanism has historically lived out this truth and
allowed for it in her various traditions, at any rate in the last two
hundred years. Consistent with this comprehensiveness has been a

tolerance of new movements or expressions of spirituality within a commitment to Scripture, Tradition and historic order, and its liturgy of Word and Sacrament. Furthermore, diversity in the way God's Spirit deals with people of differing needs and backgrounds in leading them along the pilgrim way of discipleship accords with the evidence of the New Testament writings.[37]

In the Anglican Communion, and especially within the Episcopal Church, rejection of someone's position, even with strong contrary opinions and considerable heat, does not at all necessitate that the individuals themselves be rejected, nor their identity as Episcopalians be denied. Edwards stands, in fact, within a strong tradition emphasizing that children, although not born Christians, are made Christians by baptism as infants and that nurture and growth will maintain them in that state, thus making their conversion unnecessary.

> Citizenship in a nation offers a suggestive analogy. . . . Children *grow* into the meaning of citizenship, but they belong to the community all along.
> The situation is similar with baptism into the church. Baptized children are eligible for all the benefits of belonging to the kingdom of God—love, joy, peace, forgiveness. They are responsible for whatever Christian obligations they are able to undertake, more and more as they mature. Children *grow* into the meaning of membership in the people of God, but they belong to the community all along.[38]

It is clear that this approach focuses on membership in the Church rather than a relationship with Jesus Christ. These approaches need not be mutually exclusive, but within the context of Edwards' address to the bishops of the Episcopal Church they are.

Edwards is a powerful speaker in his normal manner of delivery. Here he uses the best of all evangelical techniques by giving his own personal testimony to his conversion and using that as the basis for his argument against the type of presentation represented by Fullam:

> So, let us begin with the story of my own conversion. I should say at the beginning that the conversion I will discuss is not my conversion to Christianity but my conversion to the Episcopal Church. I grew up in a Christian home and I do not remember when I have not believed myself to be a Christian or when I was not happy with the idea of being one.[39]

Edwards begins by planting himself very firmly within the Christian community as one who belongs by virtue of his place within a

Christian family and fundamentalist congregation. The approach is in agreement with the above comparison of citizenship with membership in the people of God. In the earlier section on the place of Holy Scripture we had begun looking at Edwards' summary of his earlier religious position: "Let me see if I can summarize what we all believed."[40] We will now pick up the account where we left off.

> All men are sinners in need of a Redeemer. Their sin consists generally of breaking the Ten Commandments and more specifically of smoking, drinking, playing cards (whether for money or not), dancing, mixed bathing, cursing, and breaking the Sabbath by fishing, hunting, working, or going to the movies on Sunday. God hates sin and he punishes those who commit it by sending them when they die to a literally burning hell. He has provided an escape from hell by sending his Son Jesus to die for sinners. Those who will accept Jesus as their personal Savior undergo a conversion experience marked by intense emotion. The major point of theological difference in our town was whether a person once in grace through conversion is always in grace or whether he is capable of "backsliding." Those who do persevere prove that they have been saved by avoiding the sins that we have listed and by attending church twice and Sunday School once every Sunday, prayer meeting every Wednesday night, and reading their Bibles and praying daily in between. They also attend revival meetings that are held annually (usually the second week of August). When they die they are taken up immediately into heaven which they enter through pearly gates and then spend eternity among the streets of gold.
>
> Let me assure you that I have no desire to caricature or patronize that point of view nor do I wish to imply that it is all bad by any means. Much about the system was good and most of my childhood memories are very pleasant.[41]

Whether or not he had any desire to caricature that point of view, he has nevertheless succeeded in wording it in a most unappealing fashion. In his conversion away from that point of view to one of increasing religious skepticism, three major factors come into play. First, as we have already seen, is a loss of faith in a literalistic interpretation of the Bible. Second, in a point that the majority of Episcopalians can empathize with, there is a genuine moral growth and development in Edwards that begins to look less at socially determined "sins" and more pointedly at serious ethical issues.[42] Third is a growing awareness that visibly dramatic conversions, such as could be witnessed at altar calls, were not matched by a subsequent "attractiveness of the life of the person who had it."[43] In fact, Edwards says, "As the people in the congregation that I respected least were those whose experiences seemed most regular and intense, experience came to appear to me to be the least reliable criterion for evaluating someone's religion."[44] Indeed, an understanding of the relationship of conversion to change of behavior in the converted individual does need to be looked at and correctly understood. He mentions these experiences as being "regular and intense." That regularity should call into question the validity of the "conversion" while at the same time bearing witness to the intensity of that person's need.

What Edwards has shared about his experience of being converted away from a small town fundamentalist setting is echoed in the experience of many people who, like Edwards, have wrestled with the serious issue of the authority of Scripture, the development of an ethical sense that meets reality in an adequate way, and a disappointment in Christians that they have known in their backgrounds. Being converted away from a religious position that is not adequate to meet life's realities is only part of the story. The more important part lies in answering the question "What then is one converted to?" A secondary question that can't be answered on the basis of Edwards' address is to what extent he himself owned Jesus as his personal Savior. To put it another way, was his experience within the fundamentalist context of his childhood one that included him only by birth, baptism, and peer pressure, or was it the experience of a lover of Jesus who became severely disillusioned?

Edwards now proceeds to deal with the positive side of his experience, that of his "conversion to the Episcopal Church."[45]

> One of my best friends in college was an Episcopalian and he invited me to attend Midnight Mass with him on Christmas. I went out of a combination of curiosity, a wish to scoff, and the desire to have something to do. That night I discovered the beauty of holiness or the holiness of beauty or whatever it should be called. I will never forget the impact of the candles and the vestments and that glorious solemn language. I had no intellectual categories by which I could interpret what I saw as religious, but my breath was taken by a new vision of the possibilities of beauty and that vision I was never able to forget.[46]

The immediate content of this conversion is not Jesus nor, at this stage, that of a clear personal encounter with God, nor does Edwards cloak it in that kind of language. There is an unmistakable ambience in the worship of the Episcopal Church that makes a strong appeal to the dramatic and intellectual sides of human nature. For many, that ambience conveys a sense of the numinous in a way that less symbolic forms of worship are unable to capture. Yet that numinous quality remains without definition or doctrine and can be interpreted in a variety of ways. It is, after all, a subjective experience. Edwards' choice of language leaves a wide door of interpretation open:

> The process of religious naturalization and acculturation was far more complex than anything we have time to describe here, but I do want to tell you what it felt like. I felt like Hans Christian Anderson's "Ugly Duckling" when he discovered that he was a swan. I felt like Willie Morris did when he realized that he had gone *North Toward Home*. After what seemed like a lifetime in which my reflexes and reactions had been inappropriate for the society in which I lived, after feeling left-out and peculiar, I found a world in which my reflexes seemed normal. I felt that I had experienced a second birth, this time into a world in which I fit and to which I belonged. I felt right at home and have felt that way ever since. This was my conversion and it did mean new life to me and my life ever since has been lived in gratitude to God for giving it to me.[47]

Johnson and Malony point out that "conversion to a church does not necessarily mean conversion to Christ. The distinction is between an outer, ecclesiastical conversion and an inner conversion."[48] From what Edwards has said in this address it would appear that his conversion from "revivalist Fundamentalist evangelical Protestantism" to the Episcopal Church belongs in that category.[49]

> Charles Kraft (1979) makes the valuable distinction between *cultural and Christian conversion*. The simple conversion to the culture of the advocate does not lead to a saving relationship with God but to a "new cultural allegiance. The result is a widespread nominalism with little real understanding of essential Christianity. . . ." The history of Christianity is replete with examples of cultural conversions.[50]

That cultural alliance for Edwards and for many within the Episcopal Church is one of surrender to the ambience and to the numinous quality of worship within the Episcopal Church. That does not at all invalidate those qualities within Episcopal worship. Liturgy, symbols, music, drama, and all that goes into that ambience are not to be exorcized because they fulfill their function of drawing humanity to God. On the other hand, they are not themselves to be elevated to a place where they become a substitute for the very One they are meant to convey. One of the difficulties of evangelism within this type of context is that many are indeed drawn by the ambience as an alternative to a more personalized expression of faith reflected by Fullam and the renewal movements within the Episcopal Church. This alternative may become less and less viable as the renewal movements themselves become part of the ambience of the Episcopal Church (as they already show clear signs of being). The rapid spread of the Anglican Church in Africa, to which Edwards has already referred, is part of the reason for that change in the very nature and ambience of the Anglican Communion as a whole, of which we are a part. A representative of the Church in East Africa, Grace W. Gitari, writes:

> It is well-known that the numerical strength of Anglicanism has moved away from its traditional strongholds in Britain and North America, and that it is in the countries of the Third World that the majority of Anglicans can now be found. I have therefore made a conscious effort to speak always from the perspective of my own culture and background, since that perspective is one of which the whole Church needs to be aware.[51]

Grace W. Gitari is very clear about that perspective and states it in a confessional manner:

> My own standpoint, like that of so many of my sisters in East Africa, is that of one who knows the reality of Jesus Christ as her personal Saviour. Since my encounter with the risen Lord my life has been transformed; and in my ministry among women I have known him as a friend, a comforter, a victor and the source of all the strength I need.[52]

This very personal statement of conversion to Jesus and the Body of Christ stands out in clear contrast to Edwards' conversion to the ambience of the church. The evangelical tenor of the faith of the Anglican churches in Africa is not peculiar in the Third World. There is very significant renewal in the Anglican Council of Churches in East Asia, notably in Singapore, which is a bright beacon in charismatic renewal, and in the Philippines.

The Episcopal Church in Ecuador is experiencing rapid growth following the principles of Roland Allen. The Bishop of Ecuador, the Right Reverend Adrian D. Caceres, has pointed out that "Latin America has been sacramentalized, but not evangelized . . . real conversion to the Gospel is a reality that all Christians must deal with."[53] Bishop Caceres has used extensively the ministry of the Reverend F. Brian Cox of Sharing Our Ministries Abroad (SOMA) and of myself, both of us currently working toward a doctor of ministry degree at Fuller Theological Seminary, and others in affiliation with SOMA in the evangelization and training of laity, lay leaders, and clergy within Ecuador. The emphasis in Ecuador on conversion and personal faith in Jesus is consistent with the statement of Grace W. Gitari from East Africa. Within the Episcopal Church in the United States, spiritual renewal is firmly rooted (as evidenced by a large and growing renewal organization, Episcopal Renewal Ministries), and renewed parishes are growing in the midst of a denomination that is suffering a slow decline.

Where once it was possible to take refuge from the demands of a personalized faith in the ambience of the worship life of the Church, one very often finds that very same ambience returned to its roots in the personal adoration of Jesus and of the Father of Lights.

An Approach to a Theology of Conversion

Broadly understood, the word *conversion* indicates a "turning around" that has applications to the evangelization of nonbelievers, to the evangelization of nominal Christians within existing congregations, and to "converted" people who themselves are not exempt from that call to turn around once again in their ongoing experience as Christians. This last application is reflected in Paul's use of the present passive participle *sezomenois* in 1 Corinthians: "For the word of the cross is folly to those who are perishing, but to us who are being saved it is the power of God."[54] Even the most converted person must undergo small conversions in the ongoing process of sanctification.

The more specific use of the word *conversion*, designating an initial experience of surrender to God through Jesus Christ, has a clear biblical background that is succinctly summarized by Johnson and Malony:

> The biblical analysis of Christian conversion reveals that, while the experience is unique to each person, there are also some common elements in all conversions. These elements are (*a*) the person is exposed to the influence of the Scriptures and the Holy Spirit; (*b*) there is a crisis or point of turning; (*c*) this is preceded by a precrisis incubation period; (*d*) it is followed by a postcrisis incorporation into the Christian community; and (*e*) the rite of incorporation is baptism. Subsequently, there is always evidence in the life of the individual that his/her conversion has been genuine. This evidence includes open commitment to Jesus Christ and observance of certain values embraced in His body, the church.[55]

While this directly applies to the unchurched unbeliever, it also has clear implications for the baptized nominal Christian within the existing congregation. Although baptism and incorporation into the congregation have taken place, that in itself does not require that the individual have a personal faith. The recent joint statement by the Second Anglican–Roman Catholic International Commission (ARCIC II) clarifies the nature of faith:

> When we confess that Jesus Christ is Lord, we praise and glorify God the Father, whose purpose for creation and salvation is realised in the Son, whom he sent to redeem us and to prepare a people for himself by the indwelling of the Holy Spirit. . . . Salvation is the gift of grace; it is by faith that it is appropriated. . . . Faith, therefore, not only includes an assent to the truth of the Gospel but also involves commitment of our will to God in repentance and obedience to his call; otherwise faith is dead (Jas. 2.17). Living faith is inseparable from love, issues in good works, and grows deeper in the course of a life of holiness. Christian assurance does not in any way remove from Christians the responsibility of working out their salvation with fear and trembling (Phil. 2.12–13).[56]

It is clear from this that Christian assurance, even for the baptized, incorporated church member, does not absolve one from the call to a personal faith. Each member of the Church is called to not only confess verbally Jesus as Lord but also to surrender their will in repentance and obedience to the call of God in Christ Jesus, else faith is dead. The ongoing exposure to Scripture in the liturgy of the Church must be met by the work of the Holy Spirit, who actualizes the fruit of the sacrifice of Christ in such a way that we appropriate forgiveness for our sins through a personal response to the gift of grace.[57] In short, we must be converted! There is a temptation, however, to view this only as an individualized experience occurring at a specific point in time. Ray S. Anderson raises this not only from a theological perspective but from a perspective that has important implications for the work of missions as modeled in the work of Vincent J. Donovan.[58] Anderson says,

> From a theological perspective, there is no reason why conversion may not have its inception in a communal or group process, as well as in an individual act. . . . The authentic story of conversion is not "how" one came to be a Christian, but "where" one is with Christ at the present time.
> The story of conversion is not only a description of a past event or even process by which we came to share the life of the Spirit, but it is a contemporary enactment in word and deed of our orientation

to the goal which lies in Jesus Christ himself. Conversion, thus, is not a "boundary" over which we pass in order to be described as Christians in terms of a prescribed manner of thinking, speaking or behavior. Rather, conversion is an orientation and movement from where we presently are toward the center, which is the goal determined by Jesus Christ himself. . . . The authenticity of conversion is not determined by the manner in which this beginning is experienced, but in the orientation and direction of a person's life as evidenced by the attitudes and actions which witness to Christ.[59]

In Third World settings, where American individualism is not a norm, the communal response to the process of developing faith is more common than it is within American parishes. There are identifiable homogeneous units, within parishes, whose responses to the call to conversion can be fairly accurately understood. That will be approached in the last chapter. It is clearer in American parishes that the process nature of conversion is part of normal experience and that there is, in fact, a process visible even in the most dramatic conversion.

Ideally, the assertion of Price and Weil, that baptized children "grow into the meaning of membership in the people of God,"[60] should actually bear fruit. At times it does, and there are those who consciously have never known a time when they did not know Jesus as their personal Savior. That is not quite the same thing as Edwards' statement that he does not remember a time when he did not believe himself to be a Christian and to be happy with that idea. The former statement deals with a personal encounter with the living Jesus; the latter statement, with membership within the Church and with ideas.

We do not live in an ideal world, nor is any denomination a place where the ideals of Christian education are perfectly carried out. I remember a delightful response that indicated a serious problem in a confirmation class of fourteen-year-olds. Being new in the parish, I wanted to test the effectiveness of their fourteen years of Christian education. I gave a simple written test at the beginning of the first class. One part of the test read, "Name the three persons of the Trinity." One answer came back, "The bishop, the priest, and the treasurer." Not all of the other confirmands could name all the persons of the Trinity. It became rapidly clear in discussion with these young people that they really did not know who Jesus was and had no concept that God was anything other than an idea to be subscribed to. Certainly they had no conscious experience of the presence of God nor any understanding of the call to surrender one's will to God or of the experience of forgiveness received. On the other hand, they did have a clear sense of sin and guilt, even though this sense was socially informed rather than based on either Scripture or tradition. In twenty years of ministry over five parishes in four different states, I have found that experience representative. What it clearly indicates is that we cannot trust that young people have, indeed, grown in understanding the meaning of Christian faith. While that is not a scientific sampling, it does coincide with the general experience of Episcopal priests involved in the renewal movement within the Episcopal Church. What I was looking for was not a boundary line demarcating conversion but some evidence of orientation and direction that would reveal where each of these young people was in the process of spiritual development. As far as could be clearly determined, they had been baptized, but that was all.

The concept of conversion as a movement toward Jesus Christ who is the center, rather than a boundary line to be crossed, is reflected again by Johnson and Malony:

> A more adequate definition of conversion, however, is a dynamic movement toward a center, Jesus Christ. . . . The distinction between Christianity as a "boundary to be crossed" and Christianity as a "center to be acknowledged" has far-reaching consequences for evangelism and for defining who is an insider and who is an outsider.[61]

The issue is not whether one has had this or that identifiable type of conversion experience but whether or not one is moving toward the center who is Christ and consciously aware of him as Savior and Lord.[62] In the words of Johnson and Malony, "Christian conversion is a dynamic process. . . ."[63] The object of Christian education is to place each child in the position of a growing awareness of the meaning of their ongoing relationship with Jesus Christ and with the Father. Here there is, indeed, a boundary. We are either in the process of conversion or we are not. The vitality of our Christian faith and understanding is rooted in our experience of God. Gustavo Gutiérrez states, "The solidity and energy of theological thought depend precisely on the spiritual experience that supports it. This experience takes the form, first and foremost of a profound encounter with God and God's will."[64] Although it is clear that Christian education can and should enter a person into the process of conversion and the growing awareness of the meaning of the lordship of Jesus from the very beginning of their life, many will find the words of Gutiérrez true for their experience:

A conversion is the starting point of every spiritual journey. It involves a break with the life lived up to that point; it is a prerequisite for entering the kingdom: "The time is fulfilled, and the kingdom of heaven is at hand; repent, and believe in the gospel" . . . conversion is not something that is done once and for all. It entails a development, even a painful one, that is not without its uncertainties, doubts and temptations to turn back on the road that has been travelled.[65]

Both a turning point and an ongoing process are normative aspects of conversion for those within and without the organized church. Gutiérrez says that conversion is "a prerequisite for entering the kingdom." The focal points of the kingdom and of conversion are one and the same. In the words of Origen, Jesus is the *autobasileia;* he is himself the kingdom.[66]

Notes

1. O.C. Edwards, Jr., "An Overview of Evangelism in the Church—New Testament Times to the Present" (Paper presented to the Episcopal Conference on Evangelism in Dallas, TX, January 15–16, 1976, called by the Right Reverend John M. Allin, Mimeograph), 8, 9.
2. Ibid.
3. Ibid., 1.
4. Ibid., 3.
5. Ibid., 4.
6. Ibid., 6.
7. Charles Gore, *The Holy Spirit and the Church* (New York: Charles Scribners, 1924), 181.
8. Karl Barth, "The Place of Theology," in *Theological Foundations for Ministry*, ed. Ray S. Anderson (Grand Rapids: Eerdmans, 1979), 40.
9. Gore, *Holy Spirit and the Church*, 181.
10. Ibid., 182.
11. Donald A. Hagner, "Conversion: Our Calling to Reality," *Theology News and Notes* 33, no. 2. (June 1986): 7.
12. *Dictionary of New Testament Theology*, 1975 ed., s.v. "conversion."
13. Ibid.
14. Ibid.
15. Jer. 9:26 RSV.
16. Col. 2:11, NIV.
17. Jer. 3:12, RSV.
18. *Dictionary of New Testament Theology*, 1975, ed., s.v. "conversion."
19. Ibid.
20. Ibid.
21. John 3:1–17.
22. John 3:7.
23. John 3:4, RSV.
24. Acts 16:14b–15, RSV.
25. Everett L. Fullam, *Facets of the Faith*, (Lincoln, VA: Chosen Books, 1982), 17.

26. Ibid., 28.

27. Ibid., 32.

28. Ibid., 33.

29. Ibid., 29.

30. John 9:38; Matt. 28:9, 17; among a number of other places.

31. Fullam, *Facets of the Faith*, 91.

32. William Temple quoted in Fullam, *Facets of the Faith*, 93.

33. *The Whole Duty of Man*, (London: R. Norton, 1687), xviii.

34. Fullam, *Facets of the Faith*, 98.

35. Tertullian, "Apology," in *The Ante-Nicene Fathers*, ed. Alexander Roberts and James Donaldson (Grand Rapids: Eerdmans, 1976), 3:32.

36. Edwards, "An Overview," 17.

37. Colin Craston, "Preparing the Way: An Introduction to the Debate," in *Open to the Spirit*, ed. Colin Craston, (Cincinnati: Forward Movement, 1987), 4.

38. Charles P. Price and Louis Weil, *Liturgy for Living*, Church Teaching Series (New York: Seabury, 1979), 113–14.

39. Edwards, "An Overview," 2.

40. Ibid., 3.

41. Ibid., 4.

42. Ibid., 5.

43. Ibid.

44. Ibid.

45. Ibid.

46. Ibid., 5–6.

47. Ibid., 7.

48. Cedrick B. Johnson and H. Newton Malony, *Christian Conversion: Biblical and Psychological Perspectives*, (Grand Rapids: Zondervan, 1982), 33.

49. Edwards, "An Overview," 9.

50. Johnson and Malony, *Christian Conversion*, 32.

51. Grace W. Gitari, "The Contribution of Women to the Renewal of the Church," in *Open to the Spirit*, 104.

52. Ibid., 104–5.

53. Adrian Caceres, "Roland Allen and Ecuador: An interview by Andrew Kline," *Ministry Development Journal*, no. 15 (1988): 30.

54. 1 Cor. 1:18, RSV.

55. Johnson and Malony, *Christian Conversion*, 16.

56. ARCIC II, *Salvation and the Church*, (Cincinnati: Forward Movement, 1987), 14.

57. Ibid.

58. Vincent J. Donovan, *Christianity Rediscovered*, (Maryknoll, NY: Orbis, 1978).

59. Ray S. Anderson, "A Theology for Ministry," in *Theological Foundations for Ministry*, 11.

60. Price and Weil, *Liturgy for Living*, 114.

61. Johnson and Malony, *Christian Conversion*, 40.

62. *The Book of Common Prayer* New York: Oxford University Press, (1979) 415.

63. Johnson and Malony, *Christian Conversion*, 40.

64. Gustavo Gutiérrez, *We Drink from Our Own Wells*, (Maryknoll, NY: Orbis, 1984), 37.

65. Ibid., 95.

66. Michael Green, *Evangelism in the Early Church*, (Grand Rapids: Eerdmans, 1970), 51.

2. The Centrality of Jesus in Christian Experience

An Objection to the Centrality of Jesus in Contemporary Prayers in Evangelism and Renewal Considered

A serious objection to the centrality of Jesus in the contemporary prayers so common within the renewal movements may surprise anyone whose spirituality is grounded in *The Book of Common Prayer* with such popular devotional pieces as the Te Deum Laudamus and such classic hymns as "Hail, Thou Once Despised Jesus!"[1] But on consideration of the balance represented in both *The Book of Common Prayer* and *The Hymnal*, the majority of prayers are directed to either the Father or to God in more general terms. *The Book of Common Prayer* does give us a valid historical tradition of formal prayer, but the objection assumes that all prayer is formal. Even within formal prayer, prayer to Jesus is normal and to be desired. However, it is on the basis of the overall practice of *The Book of Common Prayer* and other similar sources of formal devotional literature that the objection to the centrality of Jesus in prayers in contemporary evangelism is raised. The objection itself indicates a common surface division between the theological understanding of the nature of Jesus and the resulting devotional practices that stem from that theological division. But that is only a surface division. The actuality is that the devotional practice is part of the theology that underlies it and illustrates the strengths and weaknesses of that theology. Whether or not one makes a practice of praying to Jesus illustrates an aspect of one's theology about Jesus. There are in O.C. Edwards' presentation several statements that give us a feel for his theology about Jesus. From his personal check list, "Things I cannot Deny,"[2] comes the statement "In Jesus God not only showed us what reconciled life is like, but also made it a possibility for us."[3] Elsewhere in his presentation he says,

> Man is a sinner and he is incapable of doing anything good without the assistance of God. Man is a sinner in need of a Redeemer. This low anthropology calls for a high Christology. Classical Christian orthodoxy does not depend on biblical literalism. We all became quite fond of saying with Reinhold Niebuhr that the myths of the Bible did not have to be taken literally, but they did have to be taken seriously.[4]

The limitation of Edwards' "high Christology" is reached in his response to Wayne Schwab, who directs the evangelism program for the Episcopal Church Center:

> This point came up in a way in a phone conversation that Wayne Schwab and I had in planning my part in the conference. I had told pretty much what I was going to say and it seemed to suit him pretty well at the time, but after he had a few days to think it over, he called me back and said, "O.C., I like the corporate aspect of what you are going to talk about, but where does the experience of Jesus as personal Savior come in?" My reply was that we never experience Jesus in an unmediated form. Our experience of him is always understood in the categories of a particular Christian community.[5]

It is immediately apparent that Schwab's question is answered with a statement that says, in effect, that "the experience of Jesus as personal Savior" is an understanding mediated by a particular Christian community with which O.C. Edwards does not agree. In fact, his reaction to that phrase, "Jesus as personal Savior," is very strong:

> I think I can illustrate this best by reference to a particular kind of experience many Churchmen have had in recent years. They have been confronted by fellow Christians who have been caught up in one kind of renewal movement or another who asked them, "Do you have a personal relation with Jesus?" Now this kind of question is very upsetting to most Episcopalians because it is obvious to them that they do not have any such relation, if by that is meant a regular habit of prayer addressed to Jesus. And the nature of the question is that it suggests that they really ought to have such a relation, that they are less than Christian if they do not have it. Yet G.L. Prestige has shown in an excellent article that devotion to the sacred humanity of Christ did not develop in the Church until the twelfth century with Sts. Bernard of Clairvaux and Francis of Assisi and that it was opposed by Luther, Calvin, and the Anglican Reformers ("Eros: or, Devotion to the Sacred Humanity," *Fathers & Heretics*, pp. 180–207). This means that the devotional tradition that sounds so normal and normative by the way the question is framed can be seen to be one of the byways of Christian devotion in its deviation from the usual assumption that prayer is addressed to the Father, through the Son, and in the Spirit. Prestige also goes on to warn about dangers inherent in assuming that "some particular devotional practice not only is desirable in itself, but must be assumed to be grounded in a right theology because 'it encourages people to pray' or 'helps people in their prayers' " (p. 205). The point I wish to make is that we use a vocabulary that represents a particular tradition of Christian living and we assume that the vocabulary is objective, standard, and normative. This betrays the provincialism of our experience.[6]

Edwards makes several unwarranted assumptions. The first is that Schwab's question, "Where does the experience of Jesus as personal Savior come in?" is the same as his rewording of it, "Do you have a personal relation with Jesus?" The experience of Jesus as personal Savior is not only reflected in popular evangelical terminology, but it is also clearly expressed as the very heart of the services of baptism and confirmation in *The Book of Common Prayer*, as will be discussed in chapter 4. It does not immediately indicate a devotional practice of prayer to Jesus, although one is logically inferred from the concept "personal Savior."

Second, even where the question does indicate "a regular habit of prayer addressed to Jesus," it by no means follows that prayer to the Father is not also exercised and that some balance is not maintained and governed by the circumstances and the content of the prayers themselves. After twenty-five years of experience in the renewal movements I would say that the understanding within renewal movements in the Episcopal Church is that one has fellowship with God the Father and with his Son Jesus Christ in the power of the Spirit and that the focus of that shifts according to time, circumstance, need, and even according to the aspect of Episcopal tradition that one is drawing from. To characterize this as "a regular habit of prayer addressed to Jesus" does not reflect the reality of the devotional practices in renewal movements. It is equally clear that prayers to Jesus are common and are kept in balance with Scripture and the tradition of the Church, so that Jesus is not ignored in a devotional style that focuses solely on the Father or on God in general terms.

Third, to equate prayers to Jesus in contemporary evangelical practice with devotion to the sacred humanity of Christ in the twelfth century is to miss entirely the point that prayers to Jesus within renewal movements today are prayers to Jesus, incarnate, crucified, risen, glorified, and coming "again in glory to judge the living and the dead."[7] Prayers to Jesus are prayers to him as the head of his Body, as Lord of his Church. That Jesus is actively Lord of the Church, in practice as well as in theory, is one of the most troubling truths that renewal movements bring to the consciousness of the Church at large.

Fourth, prayers to Jesus, if they exclude the prayers addressed to the Father through the Son, would be a deviant byway from the normal balance of prayers in tradition as much as would prayers to the Father be, if they exclude personal devotion to the living Jesus as friend,[8] companion,[9] and as the head of the Church.

Fifth, Edwards himself represents a limited community within the larger framework of the Anglican Communion. The Right Reverend Michael Marshall has written,

> There are three thousand new Anglican Christians in the world every day. That is the good news. Now for the bad news. The Episcopal Church, in the latest figures released, has now the lowest membership since 1950, and church attendance in the Church of England is the lowest ever recorded. Something is wrong somewhere. The New Testament does not speak of success, but it does speak most insistently of fruitfulness. . . . We need to speak of the love of God made known to us in the person of Jesus and we need to do this in words and deeds—and always at the top of the agenda. . . . Those three thousand new Anglican Christians come from parts of the Anglican Communion where to speak of Jesus Christ could cost you your life. Yet it is in precisely those countries where Christianity is growing gloriously.[10]

While Edwards accuses evangelicals of parochialism, he himself speaks out of a shrinking and increasingly limited context within a church that is rapidly leaving him behind.

There is a danger that evangelicals and nonevangelicals alike must heed, and that is the effect of current custom and of tradition on doctrinal understanding. As Luther has said,

> Here in my case, you may also see how hard it is to struggle out of and emerge from errors which have been long confirmed by the example of the whole world and have by long habit become part of nature, as it were. How true is the proverb, "It is hard to give up the accustomed," and, "Custom is second nature." How truly Augustine says, "If one does not resist custom, it becomes a necessity."[11]

Whether or not Edwards is comfortable with the invitation to accept Jesus as personal Savior and the logically inferred inclusion of prayers to Jesus as a normal part of devotional life, his reactions must be placed against the broader background of Scripture and the early church fathers. From the viewpoint of Hans Küng, the issue at question is basic: "The wholly personal decision for God and for Jesus is the properly basic Christian decision: It is a question of Christian existence or non-existence, of being a Christian or not being a Christian."[12]

A Biblical Perspective:
Our Fellowship Is with the Father and the Son

The life and ministry of the Church is founded squarely on the presence of the resurrected Jesus with his Church. His own promise and command affirm that as normative for the Church.

> All authority in heaven and on earth has been given to me. Go therefore and make disciples of all nations, baptizing them in the name of the Father and of the Son and of the Holy Spirit, teaching them to observe all that I have commanded you; and lo, I am with you always, to the close of the age.[13]

The presence of Jesus with the Church today gives the Church its meaning for existence and provides the power through the Spirit for the fulfillment of this gospel imperative. In the words of Hans Küng,

> Against all often well-meant stretching, blending, misinterpreting and confusing of the meaning of what is Christian, things must be called by their true names, concepts taken at their face value. For the Christianity of Christians must remain Christian. But it remains Christian only if it remains explicitly *linked to the one Christ*. And he is not any sort of principle or an intentionality, not an attitude or an evolutionary goal. He is a quite definite, unmistakable, irreplaceable person with a quite definite name. In the light of this very name Christianity cannot be reduced or "elevated" to a nameless (anonymous) Christianity. The distinctive Christian reality is Christ himself.[14]

To remove the personal experience of Jesus the Christ from the heart of evangelism is to empty the great commission of its central meaning.

In commenting on the announcement of the angel of the Lord to the shepherds,[15] Luther says,

> This faith does not merely consist in believing that this story is true, as it is written. For that does not avail anything, because everyone, even the damned, believe that. Concerning faith, Scripture and God's word do not teach that it is a natural work, without grace. Rather the faith that is the right one, rich in grace, demanded by God's word and deed, is that you firmly believe Christ is born for you and that his birth is yours and come to pass for your benefit. . . . For the right foundation of all salvation which unites Christ and the believing heart in this manner is that everything they have individually becomes something they hold in common.[16]

Bonhoeffer emphasizes this point:

> The personal structure must be outlined more closely and developed as the *pro me* structure of the God-man Jesus Christ. Christ is Christ not as Christ in himself, but in his relation to me. His being Christ is his being *pro me*. The being *pro me* is in turn not meant to be understood as an effect which emanates from him, or as an accident; it is meant to be understood as the essense, as the being of the person himself.[17]

It is clear from the remarks of Luther and Bonhoeffer that Jesus
Christ is the very center of Christianity itself, and that he cannot
be treated as an impersonal concept or idea merely to be theologized
about but as a reality who must enter into personal human experience, else in the final analysis Christ and Christianity have no
meaning. Further, Christ and the believer must be united together
so that they hold all things in common.

> I will not leave you desolate; I will come to you. Yet a little while,
> and the world will see me no more, but you will see me; because
> I live, you will live also. In that day you will know that I am in my
> Father, and you in me, and I in you. He who has my commandments
> and keeps them, he it is who loves me; and he who loves me will be
> loved by my Father, and I will love him and manifest myself to him.[18]

A more intimate fellowship can hardly be imagined. In the final
analysis, Jesus means what he says, or we have to work very hard
to find another gospel than the obvious one in the teachings of the
New Testament.

Even within the context of the above quotation the balance of
prayer to the Father is kept within Christian experience. Jesus goes
on to say, "If a man loves me, he will keep my word, and my Father
will love him, and we will come to him and make our home with
him."[19] The theme is further carried out in 1 John: ". . . that which
we have seen and heard we proclaim also to you, so that you may
have fellowship with us; and our fellowship is with the Father and
with his Son Jesus Christ."[20] There is no mistaking the meaning of
the passage, Gore says,

> The Church, indeed, of which they were the first members, existed
> for no other purpose than to perpetuate both their witness and their
> experience. It was to invite men through its open doors into a human
> fellowship which they would find to be not human only but divine—
> the fellowship of very God—the fellowship of the Father and the Son.[21]

There is clear evidence of prayers to the Father and the Son in the
Book of Acts, as well as a number of instances, such as the sending
out of Paul and Barnabas, where it is not clear exactly who is being
worshiped.[22]

There is an interesting parallel between the prayer of Jesus at
the time of his crucifixion and the prayer of Stephen at his stoning.
Jesus prays, "Father, forgive them; for they know not what they
do."[23] Stephen says, "Lord Jesus, receive my spirit. . . . Lord, do
not hold this sin against them."[24] It is obvious from this that Jesus

is at the very center of Stephen's experience, even as the Father is at the center of Jesus' experience. Again, in the vision of Ananias it is the Lord Jesus who appears to him.[25]

Fullam confesses, "May I tell you what has become the deepest conviction of my heart? I believe it is the will of God that His Son, Jesus, be exalted as Head over everything—that in everything He might be preeminent."[26] And again he says, "So I believe that worship that is pleasing in the sight of God is worship that centers in Jesus Christ and is in harmony with the Holy Scripture."[27] Those are statements that the Apostle Paul would have had no difficulty with at all.

> Therefore God has highly exalted him and bestowed on him the name which is above every name, that at the name of Jesus every knee should bow, in heaven and on earth and under the earth, and every tongue confess that Jesus Christ is Lord, to the glory of God the Father.[28]

Even though the New Testament reveals the rapid development of the centrality of Jesus in Christian life and worship, prayers to the Father retain their place especially in the more formal and corporate utterances of the Church.

Fellowship with Jesus in Patristics and Its Relationship to Eucharistic Prayers to the Father

The first-century bishop and martyr Ignatius of Antioch in Syria provides us with a significant example of the centrality of Jesus in the life and experience of early Christians. He says, "I extol Jesus Christ, the God who has granted you such wisdom,"[29] and he again refers to Jesus as "the Christ God."[30] He places this in the context of the Father in commenting on his readers' relationship with their bishop: ". . . I congratulate you on having such intimacy with him as the Church enjoys with Jesus Christ, and Jesus Christ with the Father."[31] For Ignatius, Jesus is at the very center of his Christian experience. He speaks of intimacy with Jesus as a normal aspect of Christian living, saying that we are to "remain body and soul united to Jesus Christ,"[32] and he testifies of God's plan "in reference to the New Man Jesus Christ, and how it involves believing in him and loving him, and entails his Passion and resurrection."[33] He warns his readers,

> Be deaf, then, to any talk that ignores Jesus Christ, of David's lineage, of Mary; who was born, ate, and drank; was really persecuted under

> Pontius Pilate; was really crucified and died, in the sight of heaven and earth and the underworld. He was really raised from the dead, for his Father raised him, just as his Father will raise us, who believe on him, through Christ Jesus, apart from whom we have no genuine life.[34]

What is the alternative to having Jesus as personal Savior or to having a personal relationship with him? Is it to give Jesus a conceptual place that is central to salvation without giving him a central place in our experience? The martyrdom of Ignatius is fueled by an intensely personal love of Jesus, a love that springs from his unity with Jesus Christ his God and leads him to the final contest. "For though alive, it is with a passion for death that I am writing to you. My Desire has been crucified and there burns in me no passion for material things."[35] Ignatius is able to fulfill his calling because Jesus has fulfilled his promise, "I will love him and manifest myself to him."[36]

To deny Jesus a place of centrality in Christian life and experience is to come dangerously close to the subordinationism of which Origen has been accused.[37] The accusations leveled at Origen are often on the basis of a misinterpretation of his *Treatise on Prayer.*[38] An examination of the treatise itself reveals that Origen differentiates between what he calls prayer and other forms of address to God. The following is a comment of Origen's on 1 Tim. 2:1.

> He says as follows: "I exhort, therefore, first of all, that supplications, prayers, intercessions, thanksgivings, be made for all men," and so forth. I consider, then, that a "supplication" is a petition offered with entreaty for the obtaining of something which a person lacks; a "prayer" is offered in a dignified manner with ascription of praise by some one concerning matters of importance; an "intercession" is a request to God for certain things made by one who possesses more than usual confidence; "thanksgiving" is an acknowledgement, with prayer, that blessings have been obtained from God.[39]

In his subsequent treatment of these categories Origen singles out prayer in the technical sense as something that "perhaps ought" to be addressed only to the Father.[40] From the balance of his discussion it is clear that supplication, intercession, and thanksgiving (things that we normally include as part of prayer) are properly addressed to Jesus. While this may indicate a subordinationism in Origen, it does not at all bar Origen or anyone else from carrying on a daily fruitful companionship with Jesus.

The early Church did address its formal eucharistic prayers to God the Father, as is clear in *The Apostolic Tradition of Hippolytus:*

We give thee thanks, O God, through thy beloved Servant Jesus Christ, whom at the end of time thou didst send to us a Saviour and Redeemer and the Messenger of thy counsel. Who is thy Word, inseparable from thee; through whom thou didst make all things and in whom thou art well pleased.[41]

This, of course, is completely fitting, as the prayer of consecration presents the sacrifice of the Son to the Father as a prayer of thanksgiving. Sarapion also follows this in his sacramentary:

Full is the heaven, full also is the earth of thy excellent glory. Lord of Hosts fill also this sacrifice with thy power and thy participation: for to thee have we offered this living sacrifice, this bloodless oblation. To thee we have offered this bread the likeness of the body of the only-begotten.[42]

The consistency of address to God the Father in the eucharistic prayers of Hippolytus and Sarapion does not necessarily imply that other prayers in other contexts are not to be directed to Jesus and even at times to the Holy Spirit.

Contemporaneous with Sarapion and, like him, from the Church in Eygpt is St. Antony. Athanasius balances the eucharistic prayers of Sarapion by giving us insight into the ongoing practice of Antony. Antony urged others "to prefer nothing in the world above the love of Christ,"[43] commended others for "their worship of Christ,"[44] and spoke of "the Lord who is our joy, the power of the Father."[45] Consistent with the last reference, Antony, according to Athanasius, very simply addressed Jesus as Lord and directed most of his informal prayers to him.[46] The contemporaries of Antony followed the same practice particularly notable in short prayers such as that of Abba Sisois: "Lord Jesus Christ, protect me from my tongue,"[47] or "Lord, Son of God, help me!"[48] The closing on one manuscript of the collected sayings of the fathers reads,

Lord Jesus Christ, whose will all things obey: pardon what I have done and grant that I, a sinner, may sin no more. Lord, I believe that though I deserve it not, thou canst cleanse me from my sins. Lord, I know that man looks upon the face, but thou seest into the heart. Send thy Spirit into my inmost being, to take possession of my soul and my body. Without thee I cannot be saved. With thee to protect me I long for thy salvation. And now I ask for wisdom. Deign of thy great goodness to help and defend me. Guide my heart, Almighty God, that I may remember thy presence day and night."[49]

From the content of this prayer, with its confession of sin directed to Jesus, its admission of the omnipresence of Jesus, its invocation of the Spirit directed to Jesus, and its prayer for wisdom directed to Jesus as almighty God, there is an unselfconscious witness of the centrality of Jesus in the devotional life of the editor of *The Sayings of the Fathers.*

Similarly, within the historical tradition of the English church, the seventh-century theologian and historian Bede concludes his *Ecclesiastical History of the English Nation* with this prayer:

> And now, I beseech thee, good Jesus, that to whom thou hast graciously granted sweetly to partake of the words of thy wisdom and knowledge, thou wilt also vouchsafe that he may some time or other come to thee, the fountain of all wisdom, and always appear before thy face, who livest and reignest world without end. Amen.[50]

There is an unbroken continuity of the centrality of Jesus from the era of the New Testament throughout the patristic period and leading into the medieval period. The concept of a personal relationship with Jesus as a central aspect of Christian life and experience is hardly a deviant bypath of contemporary evangelicals. Quite to the contrary, an exclusion of Jesus from the centrality of our experience and affection may instead indicate an unhealthy subordinationism in one's theological view of Jesus, a subordinationism that is itself the fruit of a nineteenth- and twentieth-century scholarship that has cut itself off from the roots of the Church.

Fellowship with Jesus in The Book of Common Prayer

The services for Holy Eucharist within *The Book of Common Prayer* follow the general practice of the early Church in directing its eucharistic prayers to the Father. This includes most obviously the collects for the church year, which follow a formal structure directing the prayer to the Father through the Son. This is not, however, the case in the Daily Office, where there is a surprisingly even balance between prayers to the Father and prayers to the Son. "Daily Morning Prayer: Rite Two" is a good example of the centrality of Jesus along with the Father in this prayer book office, which is the backbone of the daily prayer life for so many Episcopalians over the years. The prayer book office is itself founded on a centuries-old tradition that goes back through Cranmer at the time of the English Reformation, through the traditions of the pre-Reformation Church, and finds its roots in the earliest devotional traditions of the Church. Some of the most used and most popular prayers and acts of adoration in Daily Morning Prayer reflect this balance and the rightness of a devotional practice that is as focused

on Jesus as it is on the Father. The most commonly known and
memorized devotional ascription maintains this balance. Many of
the canticles and each of the psalms used on a daily basis end with
this short sentence of praise that models for us a practice of worship
that elevates each member of the Trinity: "Glory to the Father,
and to the Son, and to the Holy Spirit; as it was in the beginning,
is now, and will be for ever. Amen." [51]

A series of antiphons accompany the invitatory canticles, which
when used in conjunction with the above refrain underline at the
very beginning of the service the acceptance of the worship of Jesus
as a norm along with the worship of the Father. The effect in several
instances is to turn an Old Testament psalm directed to the Lord
in general terms into an invitation to worship Jesus that acknowl-
edges him quite properly as the Creator God.

> Alleluia. The Lord is risen indeed: Come let us adore him.
> Alleluia.
> • • • •
> Come, let us sing to the Lord;
>   let us shout for joy to the Rock of our salvation.
> Let us come before his presence with thanksgiving
>   and raise a loud shout to him with psalms.
>
> For the Lord is a great God,
>   and a great King above all gods.
> In his hand are the caverns of the earth,
>   and the heights of the hills are his also.
> The sea is his, for he made it,
>   and his hands have molded the dry land.
>
> Come let us bow down, and bend the knee,
>   and kneel before the Lord our Maker.
> For he is our God,
> and we are the people of his pasture and the sheep of his hand.
>   Oh, that today you would hearken to his voice!
> • • • • • • • • • • • • • • • • • •
> Glory to the Father, and to the Son, and to the Holy
> Spirit: as it was in the beginning, is now, and will be
> for ever. Amen.
> • • • • • •
> Alleluia. The Lord is risen indeed: Come let us adore him.
> Alleluia. [52]

The most frequently used canticle in *The Book of Common Prayer*, occurring not only in Morning Prayer but also in many parishes as the major praise selection at the beginning of Holy Eucharist, is the *Gloria in excelsis*. This canticle dates from the fourth century and has been used extensively in both the Eastern and Western Church since that time. The 1979 *Book of Common Prayer* has restored it for use in Morning and Evening Prayer as well as its customary place in Holy Eucharist. Of all prayers used within Christendom, this one deserves, by its popularity and the frequency of its occurrence, to stand in a special place as a model of adoration. The first third of the *Gloria in excelsis* is addressed to the Father. The remaining two sections are profound adorations of the Son that finally end with the powerful Christocentric confession that Jesus Christ alone is the Lord, the Most High.

> Glory to God in the highest,
> and peace to his people on earth.
>
> Lord God, heavenly King,
> almighty God and Father,
> we worship you, we give you thanks,
> we praise you for your glory.
>
> Lord Jesus Christ, only Son of the Father,
> Lord God, Lamb of God,
> you take away the sin of the world;
> have mercy upon us;
> you are seated at the right hand of the Father;
> receive our prayer.
>
> For you alone are the Holy One,
> you alone are the Lord,
> you alone are the Most High,
> Jesus Christ,
> with the Holy Spirit,
> in the glory of God the Father. Amen.[53]

Another canticle, well loved in many parishes, is the *Te Deum Laudamus*. The first section is devoted to the praise of the Father; the second section, to the praise of the Son.

> You, Christ, are the king of glory,
> the eternal Son of the Father.

When you became man to set us free
you did not shun the Virgin's womb.
You overcame the sting of death
and opened the kingdom of heaven to all believers.
You are seated at God's right hand in glory.
We believe that you will come and be our judge.
  Come then, Lord, and help your people,
  bought with the price of your own blood,
  and bring us with your saints
  to glory everlasting.[54]

This fourth-century canticle has been used extensively for centuries as a regular part of the Daily Office even though its original use was probably during the eucharist.[55]

There are several other prayers addressed to Jesus in the context of the Daily Office, but even these examples give an adequate basis for having a personal relationship with Jesus as a normative part of both prayer book worship and daily life. If it is true, as Edwards asserts, that this is not something that Episcopalians are comfortable with, then the Episcopal Church has a tremendous educational task ahead of it in order to return the Church to its roots.

The history of mysticism within the heritage of the Episcopal Church is rich with profoundly warm and intimate expression of the love and adoration of Jesus. Prayers, like the following from Richard Rolle, the fourteenth-century hermit of Hampole, are a vital and central part of our tradition.

O sweet and delectable light that is my Maker unmade; enlighten the face and sharpness of my inward eye with clearness unmade, that my mind, pithily cleansed from uncleanness and made marvelous with gifts, may swiftly flee into the high mirth of love; and kindled with thy savor I may sit and rest, joying in thee, Jesu. And going as it were ravished in heavenly sweetness, and made stable in the beholding of things unseen, never, save by godly things, shall I be gladdened.

O Love everlasting, enflame my soul to love God, so that nothing may burn in me but his embraces. O good Jesu, who shall grant me to feel thee than now may neither be felt nor seen? Shed thyself into the entrails of my soul. Come into my heart and fill it with thy clearest sweetness. Moisten my mind with hot wine of thy sweet love, that forgetful of all ills and all scornful visions and imaginations, and only having thee, I may be glad and joy in Jesu my God. Henceforward, sweetest Lord, go not from me, continually biding with me in thy sweetness; for thy presence only is solace to me, and thy absence only leaves me heavy.[57]

Notes

1. *The Hymnal 1982*, New York: The Church Hymnal Corporation, 1982, hymn 495.
2. Edwards, "An Overview," 20.
3. Ibid.
4. Ibid., 6.
5. Ibid., 18.
6. Ibid., 18–19.
7. *The Book of Common Prayer* (1979), 359.
8. John 15:14, RSV.
9. Matt. 28:20b, RSV.
10. Michael Marshall, "Evangelism and Witness," *The Anglican Digest* vol. 30 (Midsummer 1988): 3.
11. Martin Luther, "Preface to the Latin Writings," in *Selected Writings of Martin Luther*, ed. T.G. Tappert (Philadelphia: Fortress, 1967), 23–24.
12. Hans Küng, *The Christian Challenge* (New York: Doubleday, 1979), 260.
13. Matt. 28:18–20, RSV.
14. Hans Küng, *Signposts for the Future* (New York: Doubleday, 1978), 8–9.
15. Luke 2:10–12, RSV.
16. Martin Luther, *Luther's Works*, ed. Helmut Lehmann (Philadelphia: Fortress, 1974), vol. 52, *Sermons II*, ed. Hans Hillerbrand, 14–15.
17. Dietrich Bonhoeffer, *Christ the Center* (New York: Harper & Row, 1966), 47.
18. John 14:18–21, RSV.
19. John 14:23, RSV.
20. 1 John 1:3, RSV.
21. Charles Gore, *The Epistles of St. John* (London: John Murray, 1920), 56, 57.
22. Acts 13:2, RSV.
23. Luke 23:34, RSV.
24. Acts 7:59, 60, RSV.
25. Acts 9:17, RSV.

26. Fullam, *Facets of the Faith*, 28.

27. Ibid., 29.

28. Phil. 2:9–11, RSV.

29. Ignatius, "Letters of Ignatius," In *Early Christian Fathers* edited by Cyril Richardson, Library of Christian Classics, Philadelphia, Westminster Press, 1953, Smyrnaeans 1:1. p. 113.

30. Ibid., Smyrnaeans 10:1. p. 115.

31. Ibid., Ephesians 5:1. p. 89.

32. Ibid., Ephesians 10:3. p. 91.

33. Ibid., Ephesians 20:1. p. 93.

34. Ibid., Trallians 9:1, 2. p. 100.

35. Ibid., Romans 7:2. p. 105.

36. Ibid., John 14:21b, RSV.

37. Henry Chadwick and J.E.L. Oulton, eds. *Alexandrian Christianity*, Library of Christian Classics (Philadelphia: Westminster Press, 1954), 189.

38. Ibid., 187.

39. Origen, "On Prayer" 14:2 in *Alexandrian Christianity* edited by Henry Chadwick and J.E.L. Oulton, Library of Christian Classics (Philadelphia: Westminster Press, 1954), p. 267.

40. Ibid., "On Prayer" 15:1. p. 269.

41. Hippolytus, *The Apostolic Tradition of Hippolytus*, trans. Burton Scott Easton (Ann Arbor, MI: Archon Books, 1962), 35.

42. Sarapion, *Bishop Sarapion's Prayer Book*, ed. John Wordsworth (Ann Arbor, MI: Archon Books, 1964), 62.

43. Athanasius, *The Life of Antony*, trans. Robert C. Gregg, Classics of Western Spirituality (New York: Paulist Press, 1980), 42.

44. Ibid., 90.

45. Ibid., 58.

46. Ibid., 96–97.

47. "*The Sayings of the Fathers*," in *Western Asceticism*, ed. Owen Chadwick, Library of Christian Classics, Ichthus edition (Philadelphia: Westminster Press, 1958), 55.

48. Ibid., 64.

49. Ibid., 189.

50. The Venerable Bede, *The Ecclesiastical History of the English Nation* (London: J.M. Dent, 1903), 382.

51. *The Book of Common Prayer*, 80.

52. Ibid., 80–82.

53. *The Book of Common Prayer*, 94–95.

54. Ibid., 96.

55. Ibid., 117, 118.

56. Richard Rolle, "The Mending of Life," in *Late Medieval Mysticism*, Library of Christian Classics (Philadelphia: Westminster Press, 1957), 235.

3. The Nature of Conversion

The Psychology of Conversion

Any genuine conversion will reach into the depths of human personality, sometimes affirming, sometimes calling into question, and sometimes bringing healing on the level of our deepest assumptions about the nature of reality. This is not always a welcome intrusion. In the words of the poet T.S. Eliot, "humankind cannot bear very much reality."[1] Conversion has many sides. "In a study of conversion in the Bible, one always finds a twin emphasis—on the divine role and on the human role."[2] While conversion is ultimately a work of God, the focus of this section is on our human experience regarding conversion.

Erik Erikson's eight stages of human development give a basic understanding of the development of human personality that provides an open door for understanding the process of Christian conversion.[3] In the first stage, *BASIC TRUST VS. BASIC MISTRUST* lays the foundation for the understanding of alienation and opens the door for the healing of that same alienation.[4] According to Erikson,

> Mothers create a sense of trust in their children by that kind administration which in its quality combines sensitive care of the baby's individual needs and a firm sense of personal trustworthiness within the trusted framework of their culture's life style. This forms the basis in the child for a sense of identity which will later combine a sense of being "all right," of being oneself, and of becoming what other people trust one will become.[5]

But even at this level Erikson sees a sense of alienation introduced that is fundamental to human experience. Erikson does not account for this, but merely states it as a given:

> But even under the most favorable circumstances, this stage seems to introduce into psychic life (and become prototypical for) a sense of inner division and universal nostalgia for a paradise forfeited. It is against this powerful combination of a sense of having been deprived, of having been divided, and of having been abandoned— that basic trust must maintain itself throughout life.[6]

From a biblical position, that sense of "a paradise forfeited" reflects a basic and very real experience of humankind in general and of each individual in particular. While the parenting we have received may either alleviate or intensify this basic sense of alienation, it does not create it but rather builds over against this inner given. Even where one's parents are rejecting and destructive to the formation of human personality, the Lord stands ready to redeem the very real and painful human experience of alienation. "For my father and my mother have forsaken me, but the LORD will take me up."[7] To the extent that one's parents are healthy and nurturing, one is spared some of the worst of human experience, yet that inner sense of alienation still needs to be dealt with. Erikson is not entirely comforting when he says, "The parental faith which supports the trust emerging in the newborn, has throughout history sought its institutional safeguard (and, on occasion, found its greatest enemy) in organized religion."[8] Because alienation is a natural state of fallen humankind that affects even our childhood upbringing and because guilt is so easily learned and so easily projected, it is important for us in the Church to deal with issues like conversion as realistically as possible without engendering an unrealistic experience of condemnation.

There is some correlation between conversion and certain of the stages of personality development, yet these personal crises cannot be viewed as the cause of conversion.

> For instance, it was seen that the conversion experience often coincides with certain developmental life crises. The most that can be concluded from this observation is that the crises contribute to the conversion experience in the sense that conversion helps the person resolve the conflict. In no way can it be stated that the crisis causes the conversion.[9]

Rather than importing an unwarranted presumption about the potential convert's psychological health in the light of the pervasiveness of alienation and guilt and the possibility of some developmental crisis, or the level of contentment of an unevangelized person, one must understand the background and orientation of each individual. Listening and observing are important parts of evangelism. Always underlying current experience is the deeper level of alienation from God that may or may not be felt or acknowledged.

> Each person has a different starting point on the road to conversion to faith in Christ; for each there is a period of growing awareness— awareness that there is a new context, the Christian faith and its community, where he/she could find solutions to a crisis, answers to questions regarding the meaning of life, and compensation for a perceived deficit in life.[10]

Johnson and Malony propose a three-stage pyschological model for Christian conversion. In a general definition of conversion, they say that

> conversion, in a general sense, is a process that brings a person to a point of surrender to the Savior, Jesus Christ. As a result of this surrender the person is incorporated into a group that calls itself the church.[11]

The first stage is characterized as a "period of growing awareness" in which one begins to discover some of the marks of alienation from God in their own experience.[12] One begins to experience oneself as *divided in allegiance and dissatisfied with life, as having subjective tension and a sense that something is missing.*[13]

The second stage is "the period of consideration."[14] This stage entails two encounters, one with a witness to the faith and the second *when the person surrenders to the Savior, Jesus Christ.*[15] Here Johnson and Malony state a theme heard earlier. "The important factor is not that the person has crossed some culturally prescribed boundary but that he/she is in dynamic movement toward a center of faith, Jesus Christ."[16]

The third stage is a period of incorporation in which the *"individual or group achieves a new contextual entity by espousing the behavior and values of the new context, the church."*[17]

Even within the context of the evangelization of nominal Christians within existing congregations, these stages are observable, although not neatly divided in time sequence. The last stage, that of incorporation is not as visible as the inclusion of a new member by baptism or by profession of faith. Nevertheless, the results of a conversion experience, no matter how gradual, can be seen even if only in retrospect. For the majority of those who undergo a conversion experience there are often times of decision that make the stages fairly clear. Not the least of these is the discomfort caused by discovering that the old familiar gospel applies to them personally after all. That, combined with an awakening to the witness of Christians within their sphere of acquaintances, points them in the direction of an encounter with Christ. To all outward intents and purposes they may well already appear to have been incorporated long before their conversion, yet even at that point there are significant changes in orientation and often a growth in moral sensitivity.

Surrender Versus Compliance

In presenting the second stage, "the period of consideration,"

Johnson and Malony use a most significant word: *surrender.* *"The climax of the period is at the* point of encounter *when the person surrenders to the Savior, Jesus Christ.*[19] There is a wide difference between compliance and surrender, so wide that compliance becomes a block to true surrender. In a paper published by the *Quarterly Journal of Studies on Alcohol,* Dr. Harry M. Tiebout, a pioneer in alcohol studies, says,

> In recent years, because of my special interest in the phenomenon of surrender, I have become aware of another conscious and unconscious phenomenon, namely compliance—which is basically partial acceptance or partial surrender, and which often serves as a block to surrender.[20]

While the subject of Tiebout's studies is the problem of compliance versus surrender in alcoholism, his observations are directly applicable to the understanding of conversion in general and specifically to the evangelization of nominal Christians. The nominal Christian who is active within a congregation but has not encountered Jesus in a saving way is living a life of compliance to the cultural norms and even to the language of the community. Where compliance is conscious, it may often be accompanied by periodic overt hostility to the community or to individuals within the community who present the gospel in a meaningful way. Where the compliance is unconscious, the resentment caused by it is buried deeper and surfaces in more subtle ways, such as avoidance, antipathy, and repression of those moments when spiritual reality threatens to break through the shell of compliance. Unlike Tiebout's experience with alcoholics, there may be no immediate crisis that can be used to pierce through the defense of compliance, but that only indicates that other methods of approach should be used. Where the individual is facing an identifiable crisis, Jesus is indeed the ultimate answer, and we should have no compunction whatever about leading a person into an encounter with him.

Compliance, as a significant block to surrender, needs to be defined more carefully:

> It means agreeing, going along, but in no way implies enthusiastic, wholehearted assent and approval. There is a willingness not to argue or resist but the cooperation is a bit grudging, a little forced; one is not entirely happy about agreeing. Compliance is, therefore, a word which portrays mixed feelings, divided sentiments.[21]

And again Tiebout says,

There is a string of words which describe halfhearted acceptance: submission, resignation, yielding, compliance, acknowledgment, concession, and so forth. With each of these words there is a feeling of reservation, a tug in the direction of nonacceptance.[22]

The call to surrender to Jesus stands out in stark contrast over against the many forms of compliance. At issue is not the mere acceptance of Jesus as an avoidance of hell and an entry into the kingdom. The issue is simply that acceptance of Jesus is acceptance of his lordship and his continuing companionship and the resulting fact that one thereafter is not solely one's own. To surrender to Jesus is finally to say yes to his will and to put to death one's egocentricity, the old man of which Paul so frequently speaks. The leading edge of that surrender for many nominal Christians lies in the area of giving assent to truths that one already knows.

Johnson and Malony identify three components of faith: "knowledge, assent, and trust."[23] The problem facing us in the evangelization of nominal Christians within existing congregations is usually not in the area of knowledge. The nominal Christian active within Episcopal churches has most often at least a surface understanding of basic Christian doctrine. The Lord's Prayer, the Nicene Creed, the General Confession, and many other parts of the eucharist service have long since been committed to memory. The evangelical questions addressed to parents and sponsors at the recurring times of baptism are all familiar. The cycle of the church year, the lectionary readings, and the collects all have proclaimed the gospel to the nominal Christian. What is missing is a period of growing awareness in which the individual begins to give assent to the application of both the bad news and the good news of the gospel in respect to his or her own life.

> It is important that the person not only know the truth but also accept it as true. In assenting to the truth the person also sees a one-to-one correspondence between the truth and his/her need.[24]

There are strong inner resistances to giving assent to truths that will limit our autonomy. Surrender, the final fruit of assent, is not something that we can ultimately negotiate with ourselves. If at no other point we find a sense of individual helplessness that speaks of a need for God, we will find it here. Surrender is a gift of God, a work of the Spirit that we invite and with which we cooperate. Surrender is an aspect of faith, and faith "is the gift of God."[25] The faith of which Pauls speaks is not a distant and well-defended intellectual acknowledgment, although it has its intellectual side.

> The final stage of faith is *trust* in God. Faith is not a cold intellectual adherence to certain doctrines, but involves a warm personal trust in a living Savior. Faith can never be divorced from the object of its attention, Jesus Christ. It is a person-to-person encounter in which a self-commitment is made to Christ.[26]

Intellect and Conversion

The intellectual part of human nature must be involved in the process of conversion. There is a difference between faith and blind presumption. Faith is established on the basis of probabilities that make it possible for a commitment of will. Both the consideration of Scripture and exposure to the transformed lives of witnesses to the reality of the gospel are part of the data on which we make a faith decision. Within the context of the Church, denominational traditions and systems of doctrine speak to the mind as well as to the heart. For some people this intellectual aspect is more important than for others.

> Each person experiences conversion in his/her own unique way. There are, however, different types of conversion. These include the emotional and intellectual stimulus type as well as experiences that emphasize either a gradual awakening or a definite crisis. In all cases some point of turning occurs in the midst of a crisis.[27]

It is fashionable in some circles to tell potential converts that they don't need to understand, just "take it on faith." That is probably the least appealing approach to make to Episcopalians. Granted the knowledge of Christ must move from the head to the heart, and there is a point beyond which the asking of unsolvable questions must move toward a leap of faith. On the other hand, the demands of the gospel will stand up against intellectual critique. There are two sides to be considered:

> It need not be a choice of intellectual rigour and integrity or emotional and physical involvement. Both—and commitment of will to obey God—are needed in full-orbed worship.[28]

Among the many who have responded to the intellectual claims of the gospel is the great second-century defender of the faith Justin. A.D. Nock, in his work *Conversion*, summarizes Justin's conversion:

> In despair he decided to give Platonism a trial, for it had a considerable reputation. In this he found no small satisfaction: the

contemplation of the Ideas fired his imagination and he hoped that he should see God. So he thought fit to have a long solitude and retired to a lonely spot near the sea. There he was met by an old man who engaged him in conversation, proved to him that the philosophers could not have knowledge of God, and having reduced him to a condition of argumentative helplessness introduced him to the prophets and to Christ.

According to this account Justin came to Christianity at the end of a chapter of a disappointed intellectual search.[29]

In a world of competing philosophies, Justin and others like him did not hesitate to argue on behalf of the faith. They made an unabashed appeal to the intellect and often backed up their claims with their own blood. Nock refers to the third-century Christian Arnobius as one who had been persuaded of the truth by a great teacher and says that, for Arnobius, "the acknowledgement of the deity of Jesus is natural gratitude."[30] Nock goes on to chart the progress of Augustine's conversion: "Augustine found himself deeply interested in the content of what he heard. He came to the conclusion that Christianity could be intellectually respectable."[31] That is of significance for Augustine for, as Nock points out, the Christianity Augustine had encountered in his childhood was not particularly profound, which "was no doubt typical of the Christianity of Africa at the time, in which the heart was stronger than the head."[32] There is a possible parallel here between Augustine and those who have taken refuge from a fundamentalist Christian background in the intellectual patina and the ambience of the Episcopal Church. A failure to minister to the mind as well as to the heart will not touch those who have fled from a naive emotional approach. Of Augustine, Nock says, "So his quest ran its way to an intellectual conviction, and this conviction gradually acquired an emotional strength sufficient to bring him to decisive action."[33] Conversion involves the whole personality, intellect, emotions, and will. Each individual's experience will be unique and arise out of their own needs and predispositions. Any evangelical methodology seeking to present the gospel to the nominal Christian within existing congregations must make space for the whole person.

Conversion and Human Needs

What moves an individual to enter into a spiritual search for truth? Some are quick to tell us that it is a sense of guilt and a need for forgiveness that draw a person to Jesus. For a few, often those with the most colorful stories of conversion, that is often the case. The impetus toward conversion is much less focused than that for most people by virtue of the simple fact that their life experience and sometimes their age make their identification as notorious sinners unlikely. The words of Jesus remain true: "Those who are well have no need of a physician, but those who are sick; I came not to call the righteous, but sinners."[34] But the reality is that many more, at the beginning of their spiritual journey, are able to identify themselves as "sick," in the sense of having needs that can be met, than are able to identify forgiveness as one of those needs. In commenting on conversion in general, Edmund Gibbs, a Fuller Theological Seminary faculty member, says,

> Some people are converted as an immediate consequence of recognizing Christ as their sin-bearer. Others initially turn to Christ, not so much out of a sense of the need for forgiveness, as a need for strength in a time of confessed weakness and inadequacy. Their awareness of sin and the need for forgiveness come as a subsequent realization.[35]

Johnson and Malony differentiate between felt needs and real needs.

> A distinction needs to be made, therefore, between real and felt needs. People may not feel they have a need for something they really should have. One task of evangelists may be to awaken in persons a sense of their need in order that they may later acknowledge what their need is and accept grace as the answer. Most market analysis would agree that people have to be prepared to receive the products being advertised.[36]

Many nominal Christians within existing congregations live a life of relatively comfortable compliance with the societal norms of the congregation. That is common within the Episcopal Church, where there is a wide divergence of attitudes toward things that more conservative groups feel are clearly unacceptable. With the removal of the Ten Commandments from the immediate context of the Holy Eucharist, the liturgical use of the Ten Commandments has decreased in many places where it was at least used occasionally. As a result of this diminished consciousness of the Ten Commandments, systematic preaching about humanity's needs, including moral law and God's holiness, is an important part of the evangelism of nominal Christians.

Deliberate attention needs to be given to the general area of needs to provide as many points of entry as possible. The late Anglican evangelist David Watson, in a chapter titled "The Moods and Questions of Today," mentions some of the most commonly experienced needs that must be addressed, such as loneliness, self-pity, self-hatred, guilt, and spiritual hunger.[37] Most obvious within many American congregations are low self-value, a growing sense of moral disorientation, and a subtle despair emanating from the hopelessness of a nuclear future. In the evangelization of nominal Christians, a sensitive approach must be taken to the uncovering of a number of the legitimate needs that leave an opening for the entrance of faith. There are those, however, who are not at all sensitive to that kind of approach who may well be sensitive to the most fundamental need of all, that of the resolution of basic human alienation.

The recent testimony of a young woman shares her wrestling over the area of need. Most of the areas of identifiable needs, such as those listed above, were outside of her experience. She, like many who are nominal Christians, was satisfied with her life. Only one need allowed the necessary opening for the gospel.

> It had never occurred to me that I had "spiritual needs" because I didn't know what that meant. If I would have heard the phrase, I might have thought it meant a lack of meaningful activity, a lack of meaningful relationships, a lack of self-esteem, or some other social or psychological deficiency. I was not lacking in those areas. Yet I was faced with the fact that a holy and just God created me and had certain expectations of how I should behave and relate to him. I realized that I barely knew him and I felt inadequate to initiate any move to draw closer to him. He was worthy of my devotion, yet I was not capable of winning his approval. All this added up to spiritual need.[38]

From the context of her discussion of this need it is apparent that two specific things shared in her awakening: the first, a decision to read the Bible, and the second, an effective living Christian witness. Scripture reading, Bible study groups, the availability of Bibles in modern translations are all important in the process of evangelization. Equally important is the witness of other living people who will risk enough to share their faith and be patiently challenging and supportive, in prayer and in deeds, of the person who is beginning a faith journey. The importance of living examples of the faith can hardly be overestimated. This following testimony shares the effect on one man of a simple prayer meeting.

> After singing, the people prayed. They didn't read from a book or repeat a liturgy they'd memorized. They discussed various situations and problems and then prayed about the things they had discussed. My emotions began to deepen. They were talking to God and I was extremely jealous. I had never in my life spoken to God, other than my quick complaint to him just before open heart surgery. What I

felt at that moment was completely unexpected and new. I wanted so much to participate in their kind of praying. I longed to understand what qualifications I needed, what knowledge I had to lay hold of to stand there with other people and talk to God. I was an outsider looking in on all of this. I had to learn what it was they had that I hadn't.[39]

While this man was responsive to the warmth and reality of the prayers of others, it is obvious for others that compliance, by its very nature, can exist also at the shared level of personal prayer. Not everyone is capable of the personal honesty that is necessary to perceive that others do indeed have a relationship with God that one does not. In contrasting the average person with character-disordered people, M. Scott Peck says, "When a psychiatrist makes the diagnosis of a character disorder, it is because the pattern of avoidance of responsibility is relatively gross in the diagnosed individual."[40] The inability of some compliant people to face personal needs and responsibilities with honesty will unavoidably and perhaps irrevocably hinder them from entering into faith.

Confession and Repentance as Biblical Imperatives

Whether or not we are consciously aware of it, a fundamental need of humankind is the need to be forgiven. Scripture is very clear about the all-inclusive nature of sin and guilt. This is not just an Old Testament issue. Paul, in quoting from the Old Testament, makes this need the basis for the subsequent reception of grace:

> . . . I have already charged that all men, both Jews and Greeks, are under the power of sin, as it is written:
> "None is righteous, no, not one;
> no one understands, no one seeks for God.
> All have turned aside, together they have gone wrong;
> no one does good, not even one."
> "Their throat is an open grave,
> they use their tongues to deceive."
> "The venom of asps is under their lips."
> "Their mouth is full of curses and bitterness."
> "Their feet are swift to shed blood,
> in their paths are ruin and misery,
> and the way of peace they do not know."
> "There is no fear of God before their eyes."
> Now we know that whatever the law says it speaks to those who are under the law, so that every mouth may be stopped, and the whole world may be held accountable to God.[41]

No one escapes this egalitarian declaration. All alike are included, but often the awareness of this need steals up on us and catches us unaware as we begin to open ourselves up to the possibility of fellowship with God. In the words of the Scots divine George MacDonald, ". . . the first visit of God to the human soul is generally in a cloud of fear and doubt, rising from the soul itself at his approach."[42] Edmund Gibbs describes this growing awareness:

> Whether or not there was an acute awareness of the pain and guilt of sin prior to conversion, this recognition intensifies following any genuine conversion experience which has been brought about by the Holy Spirit. Increasingly we come to recognize what it cost the sinless Son of God to identify with us to the extent of bearing our sins, and with that realization our love and gratitude increase proportionately.[43]

The Book of Common Prayer provides a wide variety of prayers and approaches for dealing with the issues of guilt and repentance, from the inclusion of confessions and absolutions as a normal part of eucharist and the Daily Offices to the inclusion of a new Pastoral Office, "The Reconciliation of a Penitent."[44] One of the clearest summaries of the traditional Episcopalian approach is in the section titled "An Exhortation," which is appropriate for use on Ash Wednesday or the first Sunday in Lent.

> Examine your lives and conduct by the rule of God's commandments, that you may perceive wherein you have offended in what you have done or left undone, whether in thought, word, or deed. And acknowledge your sins before Almighty God, with full purpose of amendment of life, being ready to make restitution for all injuries and wrongs done by you to others; and also being ready to forgive those who have offended you, in order that you yourselves may be forgiven. And then, being reconciled with one another, come to the banquet of that most heavenly Food.

> And if in your preparation, you need help and counsel, then go and open your grief to a discreet and understanding priest, and confess your sins, that you may receive the benefit of absolution, and spiritual counsel and advice; to the removal of scruple and doubt, the assurance of pardon, and the strengthening of your faith.[45]

The prayers of confession within the worship life of the Episcopal Church are founded on an examination of our lives on the basis of the law of God. The awareness of our personal responsibility is not shallow within *The Book of Common Prayer*, as is evidenced by these favorite lines of many Episcopalians from the confession in "Morning Prayer II":

Most merciful God,
we confess that we have sinned against you
in thought, word and deed,
by what we have done,
and by what we have left undone.
We have not loved you with our whole heart;
we have not loved our neighbors as ourselves.[46]

The awareness of sins of commission and omission has long been a part of the piety of many Episcopalians.

From a biblical perspective, the prayer book practice rests on the promises of Scripture. Both the exhortation and the variety of confessions provided in the Prayer Book depend on biblical promises, like "If we confess our sins, he is faithful and just, and will forgive our sins and cleanse us from all unrighteousness."[47] Within the context of that promise in the First Epistle of John is this very familiar word of assurance, quoted after the absolution in "Holy Eucharist I," that states the basis of our forgiveness:

> If any man sin, we have an Advocate with the Father, Jesus Christ the righteous; and he is the perfect offering for our sins, and not for ours only, but for the sins of the whole world.[48]

The Episcopal Church does not legislate an obligatory confession to God in the presence of a priest but clearly from the exhortation above provides a way of meeting the encouragement of James.

> . . . the prayer of faith will save the sick man, and the Lord will raise him up; and if he has committed sins, he will be forgiven. Therefore confess your sins to one another, and pray for one another, that you may be healed.[49]

In the final analysis it is not merely a matter of meeting the requirements of God's just laws or even of meeting Jesus' very challenging interpretation of them in the Sermon on the Mount. The frequency of repetition of the Lord's Prayer reminds us that the goal of human action is the desirability of living according to the will of God. Hans Küng rightly ties this to a person's total well-being:

> In view of the coming kingdom Jesus preaches *a supreme norm* for man's action. It is not any sort of law or dogma, not a canon or a legal clause. For him the supreme norm is the *will of God*. His will be done. This sounds very pious. But what is this will of God? God's will is not simply identical with a particular law, a dogma, or a

rule. From all that Jesus says and does, it is clear that God's will is nothing other than *man's total well-being.*[50]

Conversion is not a matter of the saving of the soul only, but the saving of the whole person, in the present as well as in the future. The end of the proclamation of the gospel is nothing other than maturity. Our goal is to "present every man mature in Christ,"[51] and every woman, too. That maturity is not an abstract spiritual maturity isolated from human nature but a maturity, in keeping with the Incarnation, that affects every aspect of our nature. For that reason, among others, conversion is an ongoing process that must keep step with the normal development of human personality. The biblical call to confession and repentance is a vital aspect of the growth in self-awareness that is so much a part of human maturing.

Implications of Conversion in Life-style

In describing the interior change of the converted person, William James says, "All we know is that there are dead feelings, dead ideas, and cold beliefs, and there are hot and live ones; and when one grows hot and alive within us, everything has to re-crystalize about it."[52] High expectations are raised by the conversion experience both on the part of the converted person, from those within the Church, and those who look on from without, waiting to see if the conversion will be validated by significant change of life. This is especially true when the conversion is of the more clearly identifiable type of experience. Those expectations may not be realistic. James himself addresses the problem:

> All which denial of two objective classes of human beings separated by a chasm must not leave us blind to the extraordinary momentousness of the fact of his conversion to the individual himself who gets converted. There are higher and lower limits of possibility set to each personal life. If a flood but goes above one's head, its absolute elevation becomes a matter of small importance; and when we touch our own upper limit and live in our own highest center of energy, we may call ourselves saved, no matter how much higher some one else's centre may be. A small man's salvation will always be a great salvation and the greatest of all facts *for him*, and we should remember this when the fruits of our ordinary evangelicism look discouraging. Who knows how much less ideal still the lives of these spiritual grubs and earthworms, these Crumps and Stigginses, might have been, if such poor grace as they have received had never touched them at all?[53]

One of the most common experiences of the newly converted and growing Christian is the alarming discovery that after the first flush of conversion wears off, a number of problems remain. The desire to change has been firmly grasped in the initial repentance, but the work is unfinished. It is actually a relief to discover with Edmund Gibbs that, "First, conversion is not just crisis but process. Following the initial turn around when I turned from serving self to serving Christ, I discovered many other areas of my life which needed 'converting.' "[54] The gradual nature of this process is underlined by George MacDonald: "As the world must be redeemed in a few men to begin with, so the soul is redeemed in a few of its thoughts, and works, and ways to begin with: it takes a long time to finish the new creation of this redemption."[55]

Johnson and Malony present an interactive model for conversion that allows both for the work of grace and the response of the individual over a period of time:

> Finally, Paul's report of his struggle with sin in his life (see Rom. 7) is convincing proof that his life was not totally changed at the moment of conversion. It was a "growing in grace" experience throughout his whole life in which he could say again and again "Not that I have attained," "I count all things loss," "I press toward the mark for the prize of the high calling of God in Christ Jesus." (Phil. 2:12, KJV) These are the words of a person in the process of becoming—not the words of a person who has arrived.[56]

This should be borne in mind on those numerous occasions when we as converted people, or other converted people in whose behavior we have vested interest, prove once again to be disappointing. We are, however, not left alone in this dilemma.

> This interactive model preserves the power of God alongside the activity of persons. It stresses change while it accounts for the fact that conversion involves a process. It allows for growth but retains an emphasis on the grace of God working within the individual.
> Most importantly, the interactive model of conversion allows for looking at behavior more as a change of direction than as a total change of behavior.[57]

Johnson and Malony point out that "it is not always possible to distinguish the outsider from the insider."[58]

An exterior examination of the fruits of conversion may not reveal all that we would like it to reveal. As a result, our evaluation of ourselves and others needs to be both patient and gentle. What is important is that there is a change in direction in the life of the converted person and that that new direction is moving toward Christ Jesus, who is himself the very center of the conversion experience.

Harry M. Tiebout raises a related issue that gives us a more complete picture of the limitations of the conversion experience. Tiebout focuses on surrender as the heart of conversion:

> With some, the surrender experience is the start of genuine growth and maturation. With others, the surrender phase is the only one ever reached, so that they never lose the need to attend meetings and to follow the program assiduously, apparently relying on the constant reminders in their daily existence to supply the necessary impetus to the surrender feeling, at least insofar as alcohol is concerned. For a few, there seems to occur a phenomenon of what might be called "selective surrender." After the effects of the initial surrender experience have worn away, the individual returns to pretty much the same person he was before, except for the fact that he doesn't drink and has no battle on that line. His surrender is not to life as a person, but to alcohol as an alcoholic.[59]

Two things are apparent from this. First, for some, conversion must be followed by incorporation for the state of surrender to Christ to be effectively maintained. That is not bad. We are, after all, corporate beings and belong in society with each other. Certainly the ongoing process of conversion depends on the give and take of life within the Body of Christ, and rather than be alarmed at the humanity of the saints we should rejoice that we, and other imperfect beings, are included. Second, some will comply with surrender over a specific issue but will not make any substantial change in the general direction of their lives. They may isolate one problem and surrender in relation to that problem and yet have no intention, desire, or perhaps ability to move toward Jesus as a new dynamic center for their being. To all intents and purposes they have found a new deeper compliance that may threaten to block them forever from the experience of true surrender, which would raise the issue of the genuineness of their conversion itself.

Implications of Conversion in Social Responsibility

There are four ways of looking at conversion that should not be separated from each other in Christian experience. We are converted from sin. That is an obvious necessity. We are also converted to Christ. That is also fairly clear for most Christians. Not so clear in the experience of the Church is that we are converted not only from sin to Christ but that we are also converted to the Body of Christ and even further to the service of Christ in the world. The liberation theologian Gustavo Gutiérrez finds plenty of legitimate targets for his critique of the individualism and reductionism within the established Church. As we speak of the conversion of nominal Christians within existing congregations, we need to exercise care ourselves that conversion not be viewed as purely individualistic or allow ourselves to spiritualize unnecessarily the very real social implications of the gospel.

> The spiritual journey has often been presented as a cultivation of individualistic values as a way to personal perfection. The relationship with God seemed to obscure the presence of others and encouraged individual Christians to be absorbed in their own interiority in order to understand and develop it better. For this reason the spiritual life was called *the interior life*, which many understood as a life lived exclusively within the individual. The important thing in it was the deployment of virtues as potentialities that had to do with the individual and had little or no connection with the outside world.[60]

The reductionism that Gutiérrez accuses the Church of flows from that individualism.

> For example, the poor/rich opposition (a social fact) is reduced to the humble/proud opposition (something within the individual). . . . It is a frequent occurrence in the interpretation of the Magnificat— that profoundly beautiful expression of the spirituality of the poor of Yahweh—when the exegete loses sight of its roots in the life and hopes of Mary's people and, in the final analysis, in the personal experience of the mother of Jesus herself.[61]

While we should not loose sight of the legitimacy of the individualized interpretation, Gutiérrez's basic point is right. Our following of Jesus is impoverished by both an exaggerated individualism and by reductionism. We are in fact converted, not just from sin and not just to Christ and the Body of Christ, but we are converted also to the service of Christ in the midst of the world that he came to redeem. After cataloging the very real tribulations of the poor in Latin America, Gutiérrez indicates the need for personal conversion and goes on to say,

> The change called for is not simply an interior one but one that involves the entire person as a corporeal being (a factor of human solidarity, . . .) and therefore also has consequences for the web of social relationships of which the individual is a part.[62]

As evangelism and the resulting conversions of the poor within the context of Latin America involve one immediately with the "web of social relationships" of which they are a part, so also the call to the conversion of nominal Christians within existing congregations should involve us more deeply in meeting the needs of the society of which we are a part. That will include not only our own poor but also the web of society of which each parish is a part. Within the context of the Episcopal Church, the stereotypical upper-crust parishes that do exist are numerically far outweighed by working-class churches with hourly wage earners. The converted person is not converted out of the world but is converted to be the "light of the world" as he or she experiences it.[63] Conversion presupposes "that one decides to set out on a new path."[64] That new path is a path directed at once toward Jesus as the new center of being and at the same time a path of humble service to him in the world as we experience it. It is not a journey that we set out on alone, but it is a corporate adventure of the Body of Christ.

> The following of Jesus is not, purely or primarily, an individual matter but a collective adventure. The journey of the people of God is set in motion by direct encounter with the Lord but an encounter in community: "We have found the Messiah."[65]

The community of which we are a part is the beginning of the manifestation of the reign of Christ on earth. Our proclamation of the gospel, the accompanying works of love and justice, and signs and wonders of the healing ministry that so often attend the proclamation of the gospel are "an anticipation and pledge of that reign."[66]

Notes

1. T.S. Eliot, "Murder in the Cathedral," in *The Complete Poems and Plays* (New York: Harcourt, Brace & World, 1962), 209.

2. Johnson and Malony, *Christian Conversion*, 73.

3. Ibid., 13.

4. Erik Erikson, *Childhood and Society* (New York: W.W. Norton, 1963), 247.

5. Ibid., 249.

6. Ibid., 250.

7. Ps. 27:10, RSV.

8. Erikson, *Childhood and Society*, 250.

9. Johnson and Malony, *Christian Conversion*, 68.

10. Ibid., 23.

11. Ibid., 71.

12. Ibid.

13. Ibid., 139.

14. Ibid., 71.

15. Ibid.

16. Ibid.

17. Ibid., 7.

18. Ibid., 71.

19. Ibid.

20. Harry M. Tiebout, *Surrender Versus Compliance in Therapy with Special Reference to Alcoholism* (reprint from *Quarterly Journal of Studies on Alcohol* 14 [1953] Center City, MN: Hazeldon, n.d., 6.

21. Ibid.

22. Ibid., 4.

23. Johnson and Malony, *Christian Conversion*, 82.

24. Ibid.

25. Eph. 2:8b, RSV.

26. Johnson and Malony, *Christian Conversion*, 82.

27. Ibid.

28. Craston, "Preparing the Way," 15.

29. A.D. Nock, *Conversion* (London: Oxford University Press, 1933), 256.

30. Ibid., 257.

31. Ibid., 264.

32. Ibid., 266.

33. Ibid.

34. Mark 2:17, RSV.

35. Edmund Gibbs, "Conversion: A New Way of Living," in *Theology, News and Notes*, ed. Edmund Gibbs (June 1986): 11.

36. Johnson and Malony, *Christian Conversion*, 136.

37. David Watson, *I Believe in Evangelism* (Grand Rapids: Eerdmans, 1987), 19–21.

38. Ruth Rosen, ed., *Jesus for Jews* (San Francisco: A Messianic Jewish Perspective, 1987), 197.

39. Ibid., 177.

40. M. Scott Peck, *The Road Less Traveled* (New York: Touchstone, 1978), 39–40.

41. Rom. 3:9b–19, RSV.

42. George MacDonald, *George MacDonald: An Anthology*, ed. C.S. Lewis (New York: Macmillan, 1947), 146.

43. Gibbs, "Conversion," 1.

44. *The Book of Common Prayer*, 447.

45. Ibid., 317.

46. Ibid., 79.

47. 1 John 1:9, RSV.

48. *The Book of Common Prayer*, 332 and 1 John 2:1–2.

49. James 5:15, 16a, RSV.

50. Küng, *Signposts*, 15.

51. Col. 1:28, RSV.

52. William James, *The Varieties of Religious Experience* (New York: Modern Library, 1929), 193.

53. Ibid.

54. Gibbs, "Conversion," 6.

55. MacDonald, *George MacDonald: An Anthology*, 56.

56. Johnson and Malony, *Christian Conversion*, 122.

57. Ibid.

58. Ibid., 100.

59. Harry M. Tiebout, *The Act of Surrender in the Therapeutic Process* (New York: National Council on Alcoholism, n.d.), 12.

60. Gutiérrez, *Wells*, 14.

61. Ibid., 15.

62. Ibid., 98.

63. Matt. 5:14, RSV.

64. Gutiérrez, *Wells*, 95.
65. Ibid., 42.
66. Ibid., 43.

4. The Reawakening of Baptism and Confirmation

Baptism and Confirmation in The Book of Common Prayer

The Episcopalian who seeks to bring nominal Christians within the congregation to a dynamic and personalized faith does not need to reach beyond the existing tradition of the Episcopal Church and borrow an evangelical methodology foreign to the Episcopal Church. To do so may, in fact, make the hearing of a call to an awakened and personalized faith more difficult than it needs to be. The tradition of the Episcopal Church, as it is represented in *The Book of Common Prayer*, conveys a familiar evangelical methodology that is more than adequate to bring someone to the point of conversion. There are those within the Episcopal Church who will argue against the necessity of conversion and personal acceptance of Jesus as Savior and will subsequently argue against the following interpretation of *The Book of Common Prayer*. Those who do so argue justifiably on the basis of their presuppositions, as I do on mine. Nevertheless, *The Book of Common Prayer* itself speaks with clarity of repentance and personal faith and provides a number of viable methods for the individual to enter into the experience of conversion. At the heart of the prayer book understanding of the dynamics of personal faith is the sacrament of Holy Baptism and the sacramental act of confirmation. It is to these that we now turn.

The theology of Holy Baptism within *The Book of Common Prayer* is focused primarily on two aspects of the sacrament of Holy Baptism. Confirmation relies on Holy Baptism for its meaning and is included in the discussion because of the fundamental connection between the two in *The Book of Common Prayer*. The first place of focus is on the examination of baptismal candidates, and the second is on the act of baptism itself and its accompanying prayer. The second focus will be discussed in the next section.

The rubrics that introduce the actual questions in the examination of candidates state, *"Then the Celebrant asks the following questions of the candidates who can speak for themselves, and of the parents and godparents who speak on behalf of the infants and younger children."*[1] It should be first noted that this rubric introducing the questions has its immediate emphasis on personal responsibility.

The sacramental act of confirmation reemphasizes this responsibility in the bishop's questions to the candidates who, now being of age, can speak for themselves.

The rubrics introducing confirmation speak clearly about the responsibility of both those who were baptized as adults and those who were previously baptized as infants or young children to take personal responsibility for their faith.

> In the course of their Christian development, those baptized at an early age are expected, when they are ready and have been duly prepared, to make a mature public affirmation of their faith and commitment to the responsibilities of their Baptism and to receive the laying on of hands by the bishop.
>
> Those baptized as adults, unless baptized with the laying on of hands by a bishop, are also expected to make a public affirmation of their faith and commitment to the responsibilities of their Baptism in the presence of a bishop and to receive the laying on of hands.[2]

As an adult then, whether baptized at an early age or at an age when one can answer for oneself, personal responsibility is emphasized. In the following questions and answers from the sacramental act of confirmation, the bishop addresses the candidates as a group, but they, in fact, answer as individuals, not with "we do" but with "I do."

> *The Bishop asks the candidates*
> Do you reaffirm your renunciation of evil?
> *Candidate* I do.
> *Bishop*
> Do you renew your commitment to Jesus Christ?
> *Candidate*
> I do, and with God's grace I will follow him as my Savior and Lord.[3]

The Book of Common Prayer does not put forward any other concept of faith but a personal one. That is clear both from the questions in the baptismal examination and in the reaffirmation required in confirmation. But what are the questions that one is reaffirming and renewing?

> *Question* Do you renounce Satan and all the spiritual forces of wickedness that rebel against God?
> *Answer* I renounce them.
> *Question* Do you renounce the evil powers of this world which corrupt and destroy the creatures of God?
> *Answer* I renounce them.

Question Do you renounce all sinful desires that draw you from the love of God?
Answer I renounce them.

Question Do you turn to Jesus Christ and accept him as your Savior?
Answer I do.

Question Do you put your whole trust in his grace and love?
Answer I do.

Question Do you promise to follow and obey him as your Lord?
Answer I do.[4]

The above questions and answers are obviously formulated to give the individual a clear, personal, and public way of affirming a very personal faith in Jesus and, at that, a faith that evidences considerable warmth and trust. The central question, "Do you turn to Jesus Christ and accept him as your Savior?"[5] carries with it the meaning of conversion in the words *turn* and *accept*, and it is further evident from the question that Jesus Christ is the central content of conversion in the understanding of *The Book of Common Prayer*. Within the context of this conversion are the earlier questions that draw forth the three renunciations of evil and the final question, which makes the lordship of Jesus inseparable from the acceptance of him as Savior. The renunciations will be discussed in the final chapter in the section on spiritual warfare.

The Postbaptismal Prayer and Baptismal Regeneration

The wording of the postbaptismal prayer leaves itself open unnecessarily to the theological interpretation of baptismal regeneration without the necessity of personal faith. The prayer is used both for adults and for children who cannot yet speak for themselves. In respect to the latter, the prayer makes a bold assumption in faith that needs to be carefully examined:

> Heavenly Father, we thank you that by water and the Holy Spirit you have bestowed upon *these* your *servants* the forgiveness of sin, and have raised *them* to the new life of grace. Sustain *them*, O Lord, in your Holy Spirit. Give *them* an inquiring and discerning heart, the courage to will and to persevere, a spirit to know and to love you, and the gift of joy and wonder in all your works. *Amen.*[6]

That prayer, said in faith over infants, brings two strong reactions. One reaction is the view that if you are baptized, according to the Prayer Book, you are already converted. The other strong reaction is expressed by Bishop Gore:

Of the baptized who have no knowledge of the meaning of their baptism or show no respect to it, he could not bear to speak as, in the real sense, "begotten of God." To be sons of God, he would tell us, involves co-operation on our part with the act of God in us. Thus St. John would be as far as possible from allowing us to treat baptism as a charm. He would not, I think, sanction our struggling to "get people baptized" with little or no regard to their dispositions; nor surely would he sanction the baptism of infants except with a very real guarantee for their being brought up to understand the meaning of what had been bestowed upon them.[7]

Bishop Gore attacks the popularized version of baptismal regeneration on the basis of its incompatibility with the demand of the gospel for a meaningful personal relationship with Jesus that transforms the life of the believer. Gore points to a serious difficulty within the Church that stems from the vast numbers of nominal Christians and the external conformity that results from that nominalism.

It is, therefore, desperately hard to apply the principles of St. John to a state of society in which the world and the Church have become wholly fused; in which it costs nothing to profess Christianity— indeed, it rather costs something to withhold the profession—in which accordingly there are vast masses of nominal "brethren" whose membership counts for nothing in their lives and who respond not at all to the appeals of membership. In other words, we have a world to deal with of which St. John had no experience—a world which cannot be dealt with either as if it were really Christian or as if it were not more or less deeply leavened by the Christian tradition.[8]

The presentation of baptism apart from an individual need to participate in our own regeneration has left the Church in a weakened condition as the serious attrition of the Episcopal Church in the United States demonstrates in comparison with the rapid growth of the Anglican Communion in the Third World with its more evangelical emphasis. From the viewpoint of Gore, one of the things that has suffered has been the relationship of the concept of regeneration of holiness.[9] Holiness, and its application to social issues such as premarital intercourse, homosexuality, and abortion, is a matter of hot debate within the Episcopal Church today. Those who see no need for personal conversion and the acceptance of Jesus as Savior and Lord must look elsewhere than to the traditional biblical foundations for an understanding of ethics and interpersonal relationships.

The question that needs to be asked is whether or not the post-baptismal prayer in the service of Holy Baptism actually necessitates a contemporary doctrine of baptismal regeneration on the supposed basis of our English Reformation tradition. The late Anglican evangelist David Watson indicates that the problem arises from an inadequate understanding of the covenant theology of the author of the prayer:

> For example, it is commonly believed by many that the Church of England has always taught "baptismal regeneration"; and certainly the 1662 Prayer Book gives that impression when, immediately after a child has been baptised, the priest shall say, "Seeing now . . . that this child is regenerate . . ." However, the original drafter of this service was a man called Martin Bucer (1491–1551), who was one of the leading Reformers and at one time Regius Professor of Divinity at Cambridge. It was there that he influenced the 1549 Book of Common Prayer, including this particular statement in the baptism service. Now Bucer was a "Calvinist" in his theology, and in fact Calvin sat at his feet when he was teaching in Strasbourg from 1538–41; and it is virtually certain that Bucer did *not* believe in baptismal regeneration. Further, the bishops at that time who accepted this service of baptism were, for the most part, Calvinist in their theology, and they too did not believe in baptismal regeneration.
>
> So what did Bucer mean by this statement, which has unfortunately caused such confusion for many years? He was simply better versed in "covenant theology" than most of us today. The nature of faith in the Bible is that we take a promise of God, claim it for ourselves, and then dare to believe the truth of it even before (perhaps long before) the fulfillment of the promise is worked out in our experience. For example, Mary, in the *Magnificat*, praised God that he *had* done great things for her, when, at the time, she had only the promise of the angel to show for it. Now since baptism is the sign or pledge of the covenant promises of God, as soon as that person (or child) has been baptised we can look forward in daring faith to the fulfillment of those promises in experience. It may be some time before that fulfillment is worked out. If the conditions are not fulfilled, the promises will not be fulfilled. But in daring faith, based on the covenant promises of God and sealed with the sign of the covenant, we say "seeing now . . . that this child is regenerate . . ." Within the context of covenant theology, that makes a lot of sense; but divorced from that context, it can be thoroughly misleading and has, sadly, confused many about the significance of this sacrament.[10]

The postbaptismal prayer is then to be understood as a prayer of faith that is based on the understanding of covenant theology. Even a superficial survey of the nature of covenants in the Old and New Testaments will reveal that membership in both covenants was not automatically passed from generation to generation.[11] It is not unusual for a newly converted Episcopalian to be confronted by an advocate of anabaptism who demands, "Now that you have accepted Jesus as your personal Savior you have to be baptized." The proper answer to that demand, on the basis of the covenant theology tradition of the Prayer Book and on the basis of that theology's biblical basis is "Thank God that my postbaptismal prayer has finally been fulfilled and the faith of my parents rewarded. My baptism is now complete!" This approach makes complete sense in relation to one of the most commonly remembered catechism statements among Episcopalians.

> *Question* What are the sacraments?
> *Answer* The sacraments are outward and visible signs of inward and spiritual grace, given by Christ as sure and certain means by which we receive that grace.[12]

For the Episcopalian, the sacraments are efficacious but not magical. A sacrament, to bear its full fruit, needs the faith and participation of the believer. That is to say, Holy Baptism is completed by the personal acceptance of Jesus as Savior and Lord as spoken of by the questions in the examination of the candidates, and the postbaptismal prayer affirms this from the viewpoint of covenant theology.

An Insight From Hans Küng

In discussing confirmation, Hans Küng roots it immediately as a rite that derives its meaning directly from baptism.

> The basic insight which emerges from the exegetical and historical findings is that *the modern rite of confirmation has been developed out of the baptismal rite.* The rite of confirmation is historically and susbstantially a part, an element, a phase of the one initiation which was accomplished in the Church from the very beginning with baptism. Without baptism there is no confirmation.[13]

That understanding of the context from which confirmation rises is in accord with the thrust of confirmation from a Prayer Book perspective. Küng's position on confirmation removes it from being one of seven sacraments and makes of it, in effect, what we as Episcopalians refer to as a sacramental act.

> It is therefore possible to differentiate between confirmation and baptism (which, together with the eucharist, is the main sacrament) by calling the former a secondary sacrament which has a part in baptism.[14]

Küng's resulting position is one that is much more agreeable to the Episcopal Church than to the Roman Catholic Church. From this point of view, that the rite of confirmation exists separately from baptism is an awkward reality resulting from the development of church history. What is missing in Hans Küng's approach is an understanding of covenant theology that would allow confirmation to be a natural and logical fulfillment of baptismal promises. Küng's argument approaches confirmation from the viewpoint of child baptism as a deficient mode that needs to be fulfilled by an adult faith rather than viewing confirmation as the fruition of baptism. Küng's supporting argument defends child baptism on the basis of an argument from silence. "Child baptism . . . *cannot be shown to be unjustifiable* from the outset in the light of the New Testament."[15] This he supports with an appeal to an understanding of God's grace and the family contact of the child. The extent of Küng's critique of child baptism is clear from the following:

> From all this it follows that, even if child baptism can be justified in principle in the light of the New Testament and if in practice it is the solution to be preferred, it is by no means the ideal type of baptism envisaged by the New Testament. Even though it is in fact the normal case, in theological terms it remains a borderline case. Without the faith actually realized, child baptism remains a torso: a kind of civic right in the community, truly granted but not claimed. Child baptism is therefore a *deficient mode of baptism:* an inconclusive, uncompleted baptism which calls for a conclusion, a completion, in actual faith and profession of faith on the part of the baptized person himself.[16]

Covenant theology, as argued above by David Watson, provides a much stronger validation for child baptism. Yet for Küng this deficient mode nevertheless remains efficacious.

> *Child baptism destines the baptized person to faith and the profession of faith.* Child baptism expresses the essential solidarity of faith and baptism—which does not mean that they necessarily coincide in time. It does so because baptism marks out a person for faith, directs him to faith, and awaits his response in faith. God's Yes to man demands man's Yes to God. If the believer does not absorb the significance of baptism, child baptism remains fruitless. Only when the believer seizes on the meaning of baptism does child baptism reach its goal.[17]

From the position of covenant theology, Küng's argument bears full force. "Man's Yes to God" in confirmation is the rightful fruition of the promises of his baptism as a child. That baptism, empowered by the faith of parents, sponsors, and the Church, directs the individual to faith in the context of the covenant promises. Child baptism is not "a kind of civic right in the community" but the sacrament of covenant belonging in the family of God that, indeed, requires the adult to make his or her own decision and affirmation in the midst of the covenant community of faith. At this point the approach of Küng and of covenant theology come together to give an adequate understanding of confirmation.

> Historically and essentially the significance of confirmation lies quite clearly in the fact that it renders explicit what is implicit in baptism, that it is a ratification and completion of baptism. Phenomenologically confirmation marks the point, within what is naturally a long and complex development, at which the child, baptized at the request and guarantee of his parents, after a basic catechesis suited to his age, publically accepts his baptism and makes his profession of faith before the congregation. In this special rite he is recognized and accepted as a full member of the ecclesial community by its representatives. . . .[18]

Both from the theology of Hans Küng and from the position of covenant theology, confirmation must take an important place in providing an opportunity for catechesis and a formal place for the ratification of personal faith. For Küng, as for a covenant theology understanding of confirmation, the meaning of the postbaptismal prayer is fulfilled in the individual who now publicly and personally declares his faith in Jesus as Savior and Lord. Küng says,

> *Baptism*, at first received only passively by the child, now becomes effective as a result of the young person's actively grasping the offer of grace with explicit faith, with the profession of faith and with action in the light of faith.
> The *Spirit*, granted at baptism as effective power, now becomes an existential reality, determining the young person's faith and life.[19]

That is to say that confirmation not only looks backward to baptism but it also looks to the future and the ministry of the individual who is now strengthened and empowered by the Holy Spirit for service in the Body of Christ. It is a time not just of closure but of new beginning, in effect, a time of lay ordination at the hands of the bishop, who prays, "Send *them* forth in the power of that Spirit to perform the service you set before *them*,"[20] and then he lays his hands on the believer, saying, "Strengthen, O Lord, your servant N. with your Holy Spirit; empower *him* for your service; and sustain *him* all the days of *his* life. Amen."[21] Of this Küng says,

> It is a *renewal* of the event of the Spirit at baptism, now becoming effective in deliberate acceptance, in actual faith, in public

acknowledgment, and as such, it is the final stage of *laying the foundations* of a Christian existence which is proved in discipleship.[22]

The foundation that is laid, however, is not the foundation for a life of discipleship only, in the sense of learning, but of ministry in the power of the Spirit that fulfills the promise of Jesus: "But you shall receive power when the Holy Spirit has come upon you; and you shall be my witnesses in Jerusalem and in all Judea and Samaria and to the end of the earth."[23]

Reawakening Baptism and Confirmation

The whole problem posed by nominalism in faith is that the nominal Christian within the context of the existing congregation is probably already not only baptized but also confirmed and that neither baptism nor confirmation were entered into with a complete awareness and acceptance of their meaning. That, however, has been the experience of Christians throughout the ages. For the mystic Jacob Boehme, it is a matter of a forsaken covenant that he reawakens in a prayer of confession. He cries out, "I have forsaken the covenant that You, out of pure grace, made with me in baptism, in which You took me as a child and heir of eternal life."[24] And again he says, "I have dirtied with fleshly lust my beautiful garment with which You clothed me in baptism, and I lie caught in the devil's net, in Your anger."[25] In the context of that he prays, "You wish to take me again as a child and heir in Your Son, and wish to awaken in my heart proper earnest repentance and contrition. . . ."[26] Boehme's discovery of himself as a sinner is couched in terms of the loss of baptismal grace, and his prayer for conversion is, in effect, a prayer for the renewal of that grace.

> Forgive me my transgression and sin, and heal my weakness. Smash my heart and soul so that I might know myself and humble myself before You. Be my beginning to conversion and lead me on the right path so that I might walk with You. Give me Your Holy Spirit in my soul and spirit and sanctify me in your grace. . . .[27]

From a theological perspective, an approach to the baptized and confirmed nominal Christian is not the same as an approach to an unbeliever who stands outside the covenant community of God. The appeal to the nominal Christian in this context is made on the stronger ground of that which they have already received in the outward and visible form of the sacraments and on the basis of the profound meaning for conversion and personal faith implicit in baptism and confirmation. While the awakening to faith will, in its proper context, bring an awareness of sin and repentance, the appeal is made on the basis of the promises of God and the faith of the Church in the nature of the sacrament itself. Baptism and confirmation need not be undertaken again but must be reawakened and brought into focus in the life and experience of the individual.

Similarly, the father of modern pietism, Philip Jacob Spener, says of baptism,

> Your God has indeed given you Baptism, and you may be baptized only once. But he has made a covenant with you—from his side a covenant of grace and from your side a covenant of faith and a good conscience. This covenant must last through your whole life. It will be in vain that you comfort yourself in your Baptism and in its promise of grace and salvation if for your part you do not also remain in the covenant of faith and a good conscience or, having departed therefrom, return to it with sincere repentance. Accordingly, if your Baptism is to benefit you, it must remain in constant use throughout your life.[28]

Baptism is not magically active on passive, and perhaps even uncooperative, people. Baptism, to be effective, requires the participation of faith and the repentance implicit in "a good conscience." Being present within the congregation during the proclamation of the Word of God or the celebration of the sacraments is not enough.

> Again, you hear the Word of God. This is good. But it is not enough that your ear hears it. Do you let it penetrate inwardly into your heart and allow the heavenly food to be digested there, so that you get the benefit of its vitality and power, or does it go in one ear and out the other?[29]

The problem of nominalism extends even to the making of confessions and the receiving of absolution.

> This is also true of confession and absolution, which we hold to be an effective means of evangelical comfort and the forgiveness of sins. It is this, however, to none but believers. Why is it, then, that so many, who do not have the slightest bit of that aforementioned true faith, confess and have themselves absolved even while they remain unrepentant, as if their confession and absolution would be of benefit to them simply because they have performed an act, spoken a confession, and received an absolution?[30]

The old adage 'familiarity breeds contempt" is true. A lifetime of repeating, even from memory, words that have never been appropriated by faith inures the nominal Christian to discovering the reality of the person of Christ. For this reason the subject matter of preaching must include not only the Scripture but also the prayers and sacraments of the Church so that those things that have commonly been confessed as articles of faith and practice, and made a matter of intellectual assent, may reach from the head into the emotions, the will, and the life experience of those present within the existing congregation. Both baptism and confirmation must be reawakened through teaching and through new opportunities for reappropriation of their meaning. *The Book of Common Prayer* makes provision for this in one of the options in the sacramental act of confirmation. Along with the laying on of hands for confirmation, the service now includes an opportunity for reaffirmation for individuals who, already having been baptized and confirmed, now wish to reawaken their baptism and confirmation. The prayer for the use of the bishop at this time says, "*N.*, may the Holy Spirit, who has begun a good work in you, direct and uphold you in the service of Christ and his kingdom. *Amen.*"[31] This inclusion, by providing a public time of reaffirmation, gives an opportunity for a renewal of the teaching ministry of the Church, not only for the customary catechetical instruction for those being confirmed, but also for the instruction of those who have been baptized and confirmed at an earlier time without having been awakened to the personal call of God in Jesus Christ.

Baptism and Confirmation as Faith Events

Baptism and confirmation present logical and obvious opportunities for the participants to share publicly in a faith event. The key is in simplicity rather than in profundity. After years of experience with nominal Christians within existing congregations, I am convinced that the only reason why many of them have not come consciously to a personal knowledge of Jesus as Savior and Lord is because no one either explained the meaning of baptism and confirmation to them in personal terms or provided them the sacramental opportunity in a way that made clear sense to them. People are very receptive at the moments of their need of the Church and its sacraments. By virtue of birth and the subsequent challenge of child rearing, and at times of meaningful age transitions or transitions into new communities, people are open to the claims of the gospel and the real strength it offers to individuals and families. At these times the community that is the Body of Christ is a powerful evangelical tool that offers meaning and a wide variety of personal resources for the family as well as the individual. The evangelical force of the community should not be underestimated. In his challenging book *Christianity Rediscovered*, Vincent Donovan quotes a tribal elder who speaks of the force of a whole community coming to faith:

> Would you drive off the lazy ones and the ones with little faith and the stupid ones? From the first day I have spoken for these people. And I speak for them now. Now, on this day one year later, I can declare for them and for all this community, that we have reached the step in our lives where we can say, "We believe."[32]

Care needs to be taken, especially through confirmation, that the baptismal faith that is expressed is in the final analysis an individual one, as well as a corporate one. Donovan's argument is more on the basis of sentiment than Scripture, yet it makes some sense from the view of covenant theology, providing that the personal emphasis is not lost. Baptism, if it were to be divorced from confirmation, would provide an incorporating rather than an excluding evangelical tool. That has its advantages up to a point, but inherent within baptism itself is the personal challenge to individual faith and conversion that is clearly underlined in confirmation.

In the completion of baptism by confirmation every individual must say his own yes to God. The English Reformer Richard Taverner wrote,

> For baptism without faith (either of the party self, or of them that bring him to baptism, if it be a child that is baptised) is nothing worth, but it is like to a paper that hath a seal hanging to it, and hath no writing in it. Wherefore they that have the visible signs without the invisible faith, they have seals without writings.[33]

With this the World Council of Churches also agrees in its Faith and Order Paper no. 11:

> Both the baptism of believers and the baptism of infants takes place in the Church as the community of faith. When one who can answer for himself or herself is baptized, a personal confession of faith will be an integral part of the baptismal service. When an infant is baptized, the personal response will be offered at a later moment in life. In both cases, the baptized person will have to grow in the understanding of faith. For those baptized upon their own confession of faith, there is always the constant requirement of a continuing growth of personal response in faith. In the case of infants, personal confession is expected later, and Christian nurture is directed to the eliciting of this confession.[34]

The June 1986 volume of Fuller Theological Seminary's *Theology News and Notes* carries the following testimony by Daniel Brunner to the effectiveness of this sacramental system and its accompanying nurture through proper theological education in the parish:

> But even though I have not had a "conversion experience," I have had significant experiences of renewal and recommitment. My confirmation (age 15) was a very special time for me, as I (re)committed my life to Jesus and said "yes" on my own to the promises God made me at my baptism. . . . Even though I have not experienced that conversion from "being non-Christian" to "being Christian," I have experienced numerous radical changes in my Christian lifestyle.[35]

Without a supportive community to lead him into an increasingly conscious grasp of the love of God through Jesus Christ, the baptismal faith of Daniel Brunner could have easily faded into that of the nominal Christian who, like Jacob Boehme, could only lament, "Woe is me for I have forsaken my baptism."

Notes

1. *The Book of Common Prayer*, 302.
2. Ibid., 412.
3. Ibid., 415.
4. Ibid., 302–3.
5. Ibid.
6. Ibid., 308.
7. Gore, *Epistles of St. John*, 141.
8. Ibid., 158–59.
9. Ibid., 141.
10. David Watson, *I Believe in the Church* (Grand Rapids: Eerdmans, 1978), 234–35.
11. Jer. 9:25–26, RSV.
12. *The Book of Common Prayer*, 357.
13. Küng, *Signposts*, 189–90.
14. Ibid., 190.
15. Ibid., 194.
16. Ibid., 195.
17. Ibid., 194.
18. Ibid., 195.
19. Ibid., 196.
20. *The Book of Common Prayer*, 418.
21. Ibid.
22. Küng, *Signposts*, 197.
23. Acts 1:8, RSV.
24. Jacob Boehme, *The Way to Christ*, trans. Peter Erb, Classics of Western Spirituality, edited by Peter Erb and Winfried Zeller, (New York: Paulist Press, 1978), 34.
25. Ibid., 82.
26. Ibid.
27. Ibid., 83.
28. Philip Jacob Spener, *Pia Desideria* (Philadelphia: Fortress Press, 1964), 66.
29. Ibid.
30. Ibid., 67.
31. *The Book of Common Prayer*, 419.

32. Donovan, *Christianity Rediscovered*, 93.

33. Richard Taverner: "Postils on Epistles and Gospels," in *English Reformers*, edited by T.H.L. Parker. Library of Christian Classics (Philadelphia: Westminster Press, 1966), 241.

34. World Council of Churches, *Baptism, Eucharist and Ministry*, Faith and Order Paper no. 11 (Geneva: World Council of Churches, 1982), 4.

35. Daniel Brunner in, "Conversion: Five in the Process," in *Theology, News and Notes*, 33, no. 2. ed. Edmund Gibbs, (June 1986): 6.

5. The Eucharist as a Focal Point for New Birth

The Eucharist as a Structure for Evangelism

The 1979 revision of *The Book of Common Prayer*, while engendering fierce debate in some areas of the Episcopal Church, has in much of the Church been accepted. Some of the debate is focused on the reemphasis of eucharist as "the principle act of Christian worship on the Lord's Day."[1] As a result of this reemphasis of an old historical position, the Episcopal Church is becoming increasingly eucharistically centered. The use of Morning Prayer as the main worship service on Sundays still persists in some areas. From the standpoint of evangelism, Holy Eucharist is, in fact, a much more obviously usable tool for bringing people to faith. When Morning Prayer is substituted for the service of "The Word of God," it is actually necessary to stipulate that this is done "provided that a lesson from the Gospel is always included,"[2] because it is theoretically possible to make Morning Prayer almost neutral for evangelical purposes by the exclusion of the specifically christological canticles and by avoiding lectionary readings that could possibly be challenging. In fact, some synagogue services, by virtue of the use of messianic passages, could potentially provide a stronger basis for evangelism than Morning Prayer when neither christological canticles nor Gospel reading is used.

As any Episcopalian is aware, there is a great deal of flexibility in the structure of the Holy Eucharist, with a basic option between traditional language and contemporary language as well as four alternate consecration prayers for the contemporary language version. The remarks that follow in this chapter could apply to any of those options, as well as to the 1928 Prayer Book, which preceded the current book.

The Holy Eucharist is by its very nature and structure a proclamation of the gospel of our Lord Jesus Christ. The vitality of the sacrament of Holy Eucharist is itself of saving power.

> That the sacraments have power to convert should never be doubted: the conversion of Charles Simeon as a result of an obligation to attend Holy Communion in his college chapel is proof enough of this fact![3]

77

While that remains true, "the work of renewal is the work of the Holy Spirit."[4] The power of the eucharist finds its source in the Holy Spirit and in the faithfulness and prayers of the gathered congregation, which celebrates the Lord's death with faith in his saving grace. "For it is by the invocation of the Spirit that the Church lives in every aspect of its being."[5] That "epiclesis (invocation of the Spirit) has a special meaning in the Eucharist,"[6] where it stands at the central point of the consecration of the bread and wine as the Body and Blood of the Christ. For us, at the very least, Christ is really present in the eucharist, calling men and women to himself.

The two major sections of Holy Eucharist, "The Word of God" and "The Holy Communion," find as their focal point the Gospel itself. In the first section of Holy Eucharist, called "The Word of God," the sermon follows immediately on the obligatory reading of the Gospel without an intervening hymn or canticle in order to emphasize that the Gospel is the basis of the proclamation. The sermon is then followed by the Nicene Creed, which rehearses, in a systematic confession, the major elements of the faith of the gospel. Both the Nicene Creed and the earlier Apostles' Creed follow the outline of the preaching of the apostles in the Book of Acts and in early biblical formulations such as 1 Cor. 15:3–5. The main intent of this section, "The Word of God," is to highlight the gospel, which is the good news of Jesus Christ. A variety of homiletical approaches may be used in the proclamation of the gospel. Expositional, exegetical, and topical sermon methods, among others, can prepare the nominal Christians within the worshiping congregation for a saving encounter with Christ. Especially useful for Episcopalians are sermons interpreting the liturgy, history, and theological traditions of the Church. The call to conversion is clear within the framework already known to Episcopalians and often only needs to be highlighted and explained. Whatever approach is used, the intent of the sermon should be clear, that is, to present us all, priest and people alike, mature in Christ Jesus. In the words of the Scots preacher George MacDonald,

> We too must have life in ourselves. We too must, like the Life Himself, live. We can live in no way but that in which Jesus lived, in which life was made in Him. The way is, to give up our life. . . . Till then we are not alive; life is not made in us. The whole strife and labor and agony of the Son with every man is to get him to die as He died. All preaching that aims not at this is a building with wood, and hay, and stubble.[7]

For the preaching of the gospel to be effective in the preparation of the individual for conversion, the work of the Holy Spirit is paramount. This is true whether the proclamation is in the form of a sermon, a lection, or the drama and words of the eucharist itself.

> The Holy Spirit is God's means of causing the Word to have its saving impact on the person. Without the Holy Spirit the Scriptures do not come alive to the person and speak directly to his/her need. . . . The mind unaided by the Spirit does not have the facility even to begin to arrive at a preliminary understanding of the Word of God.[8]

The prayers of the priest and other members of the congregation who seek to bring to faith the nominal Christian within the congregation are a vital aspect of the release of the power of the Holy Spirit in the midst of the congregation. The more vital the connection between the worshipers and their Lord during both "The Word of God" and "The Holy Communion," the more powerful will be the proclamation of the gospel through the entirety of the Holy Eucharist.

"The Word of God" customarily concludes with the general confession. The forms provided allow for a period of silence between the invitation to confession and the confession itself. The confession is followed by an absolution. Either in the sermon, or perhaps at the time of confession itself, an explanation can be made focusing the confession not only on its general application, but on its necessary personal application. It is often helpful to recommend that the suggested period of silence following the invitation to confession be used for the personal confession of those things for which the individual may feel some guilt and then to emphasize that the confession and the absolution, if asked and received in faith, is a way to receive Jesus as personal Savior. While some do come to faith this way, others may still need to be led individually and in a person-to-person manner in a simple prayer of repentance and the acceptance of Jesus as Savior. There is a simple method of doing this during the regular pattern of eucharistic worship that, although touched on in the next paragraph, will be explained in detail later in the final section of this chapter.

"The Holy Communion" begins with "The Great Thanksgiving." The eucharistic prayer, no matter which option is used, follows the ancient pattern instituted by Jesus in the synoptic Gospels,[9] echoed by Paul.[10] The Body of Christ is given to us, and the Blood of

Christ is shed for us and "for many for the forgiveness of sins."[11]
Each individual member literally goes forward to the altar to receive
personally the Body and Blood of Christ at the altar rail. This
strongly symbolic image of the personal acceptance of Jesus as Savior
is a wonderful evangelical tool that can be used to bring people
to faith through instruction and through leading willing individuals
in prayer at this time. Again, the actual way of handling this will
be reserved for the final section of this chapter.

The words and actions that comprise "The Holy Communion"
are themselves nothing other than a very direct proclamation of
the gospel. A useful teaching device to focus the meaning of this
sacrament is an instructed eucharist, which can include not only
background historical and theological material relevant to the
eucharist in general but can be utilized as an effective method for
bringing nominal Christians within the existing congregation to a
conscious acceptance of Jesus as Savior and Lord.

Holy Eucharist and the Healing Ministry

Salvation is concerned with the whole person: body, soul, and spirit.
The New Testament word for salvation, *sōteria*, and its verb form,
sōzo, is alike for both the concepts of salvation and healing.[12] It is
not surprising to find that in the early Church the ministry of healing was included in the sacrament of salvation, the Holy Eucharist.
The theology of the healing power of the eucharist is clearly stated
by Bishop Sarapion, an Egyptian contemporary of Athanasius:

> O God of truth, let thy holy Word come upon this bread . . . that
> the bread may become the body of the Word, and upon this cup that
> the cup may become blood of the Truth; and make all who communi-
> cate to receive a medicine of life for the healing of every sickness and
> for the strengthening of all advancement and virtue, not for condem-
> nation, O God of Truth, and not for censure and reproach.[13]

The consecrated eucharistic elements are themselves a "medicine
of life" that only need to be focused on the healing of the whole
lives of the members of the congregation. In accordance with the
meaning of the Greek word for salvation as being the healing of
the whole person, including physical healing,[14] the eucharistic
prayers of Sarapion not only include the invocation above but go
on to include a provision for the laying on of hands for the sick at
the time of the offertory and an accompanying prayer:[15]

> O Lord God of compassions, stretch out thine hand and grant that

all the sick may be healed. Grant them to be counted worthy of health. Free them from the sickness which lies upon them. Let them be healed in the name of thy only-begotten. May his holy name be to them a medicine for health and soundness, because through him to thee (is) the glory and the strength in holy Spirit both now and to all the ages of ages. Amen.[16]

Another early work, *The Apostolic Tradition of Hippolytus*, also contains a blessing of oil, at the time of the offertory, for the anointing and healing of the sick.[17] It has long been the custom of the healing ministry within the Episcopal Church to use anointing with oil as part of the administration of prayers for healing, and where more appropriately than during the Eucharist itself? A basic principle of the healing ministry has always been "never to deny prayer for healing to anyone who asks for it."[18] It is self-evident that all requests for healing are not explicitly verbal in nature.

The Incorporation of the Ministry of Healing within the Eucharist

It was a pastoral event that taught me the significance of the incorporation of the ministry of healing with Holy Eucharist. A number of years ago when administering the bread at the altar rail when people were receiving communion, I noticed an expression of pain on the face of one of the older members of the congregation. I had just finished placing the bread in her right hand. Customarily, Episcopalians place their right hand over their left hand and hold their hands up to receive the bread. I was aware that this woman had had a misadventure with a large dog the day before. The dog had bitten completely through the fleshy part of her left hand between the thumb and the index finger. The right hand covered the left so that I would not have noticed the injury except for the expression on her face. As a pastor I could not pass a friend by in evident pain without doing something. Almost by reflex action I placed a hand on her head and, in simple direct words, asked God to heal her. She testified later that by the time she had returned to her seat, the pain, swelling, and discoloration had left her hand and that, further, the next day the only sign of the injury that remained was a small scab. My action, which was a response of compassion for a friend, was completely appropriate and fit in with the normal pattern of eucharistic worship without being cumbersome or awkward. It also was in harmony with the practice of the early Church in Egypt as reflected in Sarapion.

My subsequent experience, in two other parishes over a span of
ten years, is that congregations, regardless of their state of renewal,
respond well to the incorporation of healing as a normal part of
eucharist if it is explained well and done without undue emotional
pressuring or unnecessary showmanship. People in general are
responsive to love, and love is the essence of the healing ministry.

Care should be taken to introduce such a healing ministry with
adequate biblical teaching and a common sense approach that
allows the members of the congregation to express their doubts,
anxieties, and sometimes their misunderstanding of the healing
ministry. It is important to avoid inducing guilt over the fact that
not everybody is healed and that some healings by nature are slow
and reflect an ongoing process in which those who share in the
prayers for healing grow in faith and understanding of the healing
ministry. Nominal Christians and others within settings like the
Episcopal Church are apt to ask questions like "Why are some
healed and others not?" They are more relieved to hear the admission that one doesn't know than to receive a simplistic or pat answer.
Concern is also raised over the relationship of medicine to the
healing ministry. Episcopalians are less wary than some other
denominational groups about receiving illumination from the
Apocrypha. A very helpful passage from "The Wisdom of Jesus the
Son of Sirach" reads,

> Honor the physician with the honor due him . . . for the Lord created
> him; for healing comes from the Most High. . . . The Lord created
> medicines from the earth, and a sensible man will not despise them.
> . . . My son, when you are sick do not be negligent, but pray to the
> Lord, and he will heal you. . . . And give the physician his place,
> for the Lord created him; let him not leave you, for there is need
> of him. There is a time when success lies in the hands of physicians,
> for they too will pray to the Lord that he should grant them success
> in diagnosis and in healing, for the sake of preserving life. (38:1, 2,
> 4, 9, 12–14, RSV)[19]

As intimated earlier, the simplest and perhaps most suitable time
for praying for people for healing during the eucharist is when they
come to the altar rail to receive communion. During the announce-
ments, or immediately after the invitation to communion in the
section "The Breaking of the Bread," an invitation and brief
instruction can be given. If the exercise of the ministry of healing
has been introduced adequately in sermons and reinforced with
simple explanations during the announcement period, all that needs

to be done here is to invite the people to raise their right hand immediately before receiving the bread. When the celebrant or assisting minister sees a raised hand, he should simply ask what the person wants to be prayed for, then lay a hand on his or her head, or anoint with oil, and pray a simple confident prayer for healing in the name of Jesus. It is not necessary for people to be worked up emotionally for healing to ensue. As John Wimber says, "During the time of prayer for healing I encourage people to 'dial down,' that is to relax and resist becoming worked up emotionally."[20] A simple prayer in faith is all that is necessary. There are other settings where it is appropriate to take more time, but this is adequate for the eucharistic setting.

> One of the most significant ways to increase faith for healing is worship. As we draw close to God his Spirit works in us. Because church gatherings include open, corporate worship, they can be powerful environments for healing. Most church meetings are for worship, the sacraments, and the proclamation of God's word—all three of which, incidentally, may lead to healing and other works of God.[21]

The Priest and the People as Channels of Healing

The biggest anxiety about the incorporation of the healing ministry into the eucharist that Episcopalians have evidenced in the parishes that I have served in is one of a simple personal concern. The primary unspoken question goes, "If someone beside me at the altar rail is receiving the laying on of hands, what am I supposed to do?" A secondary anxiety could be similarly stated: "What if the person beside me is requesting prayer for something very personal, then what do I do if I overhear it?" The answers that I give to these questions are repeated frequently when reintroducing the prayers for healing at the altar rail during the announcement period. The frequent repetition provides a sense of security for members of the congregation that is very necessary for their personal worship to continue unhindered. In addressing the issues, I state the questions above as though they had been addressed to me verbally, saying something like, "There are two questions that may be on your mind about our prayers for healing . . ."

Because the answer to the second question is simpler, I proceed to address it first, explaining that most people will not divulge terribly personal information in that setting, nor do they need to. Those who want me to know some personal details not for public knowledge can tell me their need before the service, and when I pray for them I can pray an informed prayer that does not betray anything potentially embarrassing. If by chance those nearby do hear something that is very personal, they should understand two things. First, the person who has divulged the personal information within their hearing has done so knowing that they were present, and that is a sign of considerable trust, and second, that trust needs to be rewarded with strict confidentiality.

The first question, in which the person beside the person at the altar rail is anxious over what they are supposed to do, is answered by the presentation of the following options. I usually say, "If the person beside you is receiving the laying on of hands for healing, there are several things you can do. If you are comfortable with it, you can stretch forth your hand and place it on their shoulder and by faith participate in the prayer. If you do this, picture the power of God flowing through you like a beam of light and focusing on the area that is being prayed for. Second, if you are not sure whether or not God heals but you care for the person being prayed for, you may demonstrate that by stretching forth a hand and also placing it on the shoulder of the person being prayed for. If nothing else, the healing ministry with the laying on of hands is a demonstration of love, and love is very powerful. Third, no one is required to share in the laying on of hands. Not every person is comfortable with a public demonstration of affection, nor do they need to be. You may share in the prayer by joining your heart to it without sharing in the laying on of hands. Fourth, if you are uncomfortable with the whole idea and dislike it, I suggest that you pray for me and for yourself, and focus your own worship on the receiving of your communion."

The theological basis of the explanation in part comes from Teilhard de Chardin, who wrote, "Love is the most universal, the most formidable, and the most mysterious of cosmic energies."[22] Love is itself a cosmic energy, and in the healing ministry we connect with the love of Christ and open ourselves as channels so that his healing love may flow through us like light or electric energy. The concept of visualizing God's healing power is drawn from the excellent writings of Agnes Sanford, the wife of an Episcopal priest.[23] Her work *The Healing Light* is foundational for an understanding of the ministry of healing within an Episcopal setting.

A function of the eucharist not normally recognized is manifested at times like these, in which the eucharist itself serves the function of bringing the thoughts and attitudes of each individual and of the gathered people into judgment. This function of the eucharist is discussed by Donovan:

> The dancers of another tribe, which began to be evangelized shortly after the Masai tribe, did a very interesting thing during the Mass in their area. This was the Sonjo tribe and they were very expert dancers. They brought their music directly to the place where the bread and wine were later to be blessed, and performed it there deliberately and carefully. Some of their music was decidedly secular. The elders in that community pointed out to me that the purpose of such a procedure was to make an actual judgment on a very important area of their lives. The time of the eucharist was the time for that judgment. They were not ashamed of that particular dance in their own lives, so they wanted that part of their lives to be offered with the eucharist. There were some dances they were ashamed to bring into the eucharist. By the very fact, a judgment had been made on them. Such dances should no longer be part of their lives at all. Eucharist served as judgment for them.[24]

There are two applications to be drawn from this. First, the time of eucharist is a time of offering ourselves to God, and this offering needs to be the offering of the body as well as the soul and spirit. "I appeal to you therefore, brethren, by the mercies of God, to present your bodies as a living sacrifice, holy and acceptable to God, which is your spiritual worship."[25]

This offering is the offering of the whole person, with all the ailments to which we as human beings are prone. The offering is fittingly made in the eucharist where we tap most powerfully the redemptive grace of the sacrifice of the Christ. Second, the eucharist does indeed act as judgment on our thoughts and actions regarding others and their need of healing in so many areas of their lives. That is simply because the eucharist is, in part, an enactment of the Word of God as well as a participation in the sufferings of the Christ.

> For the word of God is living and active, sharper than any two-edged sword, piercing to the division of soul and spirit, of joints and marrow, and discerning the thoughts and intentions of the heart. And before him no creature is hidden, but all are open and laid bare to the eyes of him with whom we have to do.[26]

Having been an Episcopal priest for almost twenty years, I am acutely aware that not every priest will feel able or worthy to initiate such a ministry. I have already indicated the works of Agnes Sanford as a most valuable tool for Episcopalians. Another Episcopalian, the Reverend Morton Kelsey, has written a number of helpful books, including *Healing and Christianity*,[27] as has also the Reverend Emily Gardiner Neal,[28] a deacon within the Episcopal Church, who has for a number of years exercised a well-respected healing ministry. Also helpful for Episcopalians are the writings of a Roman Catholic priest, the Reverend Francis MacNutt.[29]

In ourselves, none of us is actually worthy to exercise this ministry, or any other, apart from the mercy and grace of God. But in Christ, by virtue of our priesthood, we are obligated by our call and ordination to exercise a very extensive ministry.

> As a priest, it will be your task to proclaim by word and deed the Gospel of Jesus Christ, and to fashion your life in accordance with its precepts. You are to love and serve the people among whom you work, caring alike for young and old, strong and weak, rich and poor. You are to preach, to declare God's forgiveness to penitent sinners, to pronounce God's blessing, to share in the administration of Holy Baptism and in the celebration of the mysteries of Christ's Body and Blood, and to perform the other ministrations entrusted to you.[30]

Among those "other ministrations" is the "Ministration to the Sick" in *The Book of Common Prayer*, which provides a eucharistic structure for the healing ministry as well as a number of other independent prayers.[31] The ministry of healing is pointedly an obligation of parish rectors and others for whom the "Celebration of a New Ministry" is appropriate.[32] These are presented with oil or some other symbol and exhorted to "use this *oil*, and be among us as a healer and reconciler."[33] While this obviously does refer to the work of reconciliation, it also applies to the healing ministry. To exclude either facet is an unnecessary reductionism.

The Effect of the Ministry of Healing on the Discovery of Faith in the Participating Congregation

Just as the thoughts of the heart are uncovered at times when the power of Christ is called upon and the risks of faith are taken, so also there is an increase of faith that comes from the very challenge and exercise of faith. Not only that, but the evident demonstration of faith and the risks of praying publicly for healing are often instrumental in preparing nominal Christians for faith decisions. John Wimber points out,

> Jesus used a show, tell, deploy, and supervise method of training. After calling the disciples he took them along with him, teaching and healing the sick as he went. Then, after he thought the disciples had seen and learned enough to try for themselves, he commissioned,

empowered, instructed and sent them out to do the same things (Matt. 10:1, 5–8).[34]

When were the apostles truly converted? That is a difficult question if one views conversion as a barrier to be crossed rather than as a continuing redirection of life. The apostles were in the process of conversion. During the ministry of Jesus they had not yet encountered the death and resurrection of Jesus, nor had they been empowered by the Holy Spirit in the sense of Acts chapter 2. They were, at best, partially informed learners who followed Jesus with mixed motives and for a variety of reasons. Regardless of their understanding and lack of sophistication in matters of faith, every nominal Christian who ventures to lay a hand on someone at the altar rail during a time of prayer for healing, even if they do so out of love and not out of faith, becomes by that action a disciple, a learner who can potentially grow in faith. That, indeed, is my experience, even within parish settings that are normally resistant to the concept of conversion and the personal acceptance of Jesus as Savior and Lord. By being inclusive rather than exclusive at this point, the way is opened for the discovery of faith, and the way is further opened for the continuing growth of faith as those previously skeptical begin to venture faith because they care for the person being prayed for. For this reason the incorporation of the ministry of healing within the eucharist is a powerful tool for the evangelism of nominal Christians within the existing congregation. That faith will be deepened as the ministry of healing in that context begins to bear fruit in actual healings, whether those healings are slow or sudden.

This approach differs, by virtue of its inclusiveness, from that of John Wimber, who opens the healing ministry up to the shared participation of people who have evident faith.

> Whenever I pray for the sick I always look among those present for the people who have faith—other members of the healing team, the person being prayed for, relatives (even children, who usually have great faith for healings), friends, and, of course, myself. When I recognize them, I instruct them to place their hands on or near the part of the body that needs healing, then I ask God to release his healing power.[35]

At the other polarity from those who have faith, Wimber warns us correctly of the negative faith of emphatically disbelieving people.

> I have been in many situations where an emotional atmosphere

created by friends and family members present has quenched faith for healing. They are so desperate and full of fear and anxiety that it is difficult for me or the person I am praying for to have much faith in healing. I usually ask them to leave, allowing only those who know how to pray and are not caught up emotionally in the situation to remain. I suspect Jesus took aside the deaf and mute man for the same reasons.[36]

Even though that is appropriate in some situations, it is neither appropriate nor necessary in the context of prayers for healing within the eucharist. There is a broad middle ground where people have neither strong faith nor strong disbelief. That broad area is the area in which the ministry of healing within the eucharist operates. While there are always some within most congregations who do indeed disbelieve, that is true of every situation where evangelism is appropriate. In a section titled "Power Evangelism," Wimber notes,

Another reason for praying for the sick is that healing aids evangelism. It is a "gospel advancer." I learned this from the Third World students who were enrolled in the School of World Mission at Fuller Theological Seminary. While their reports of individual healings were interesting, the resultant church growth and spiritual maturity were staggering. The Third World students at Fuller claimed it is easier to pray for people's healing than to tell them about Christ. In fact, they said, it is very easy to tell people about Christ *after* they have been healed. Scripture verifies this; notice how Christ frequently first healed the sick, then proclaimed the gospel of the kingdom of God.[37]

The major difference between Wimber's position and mine in this regard is my stated preference for having anyone who is willing, if only out of love and not out of faith, to share in the ministry of the laying on of hands at the altar rail. While occasionally the ministry of healing may suffer according to Wimber's warning, the overall effect is very positive.

There stands out in my memory one woman out of many nominal Christians who had a healthy skepticism over the exercise of the healing ministry. As a Unitarian who only attended periodically with her husband, her immediate theological presuppositions did not lend themselves to the acceptance of Jesus as Savior. Over the course of a year and a half I watched her discomfort as those around her received prayers of healing. Then one day as she rose from her knees after receiving communion I watched her pause behind the person I was praying for, hesitate, then step up and lay a hand on the shoulder of the person in question. It was a step of faith and experimentation, that was soon to be followed by her personal acceptance of Jesus as Savior and Lord. That scene is enacted in many ways as the ministry of healing is exercised within the congregation.

Receiving Communion during Eucharist as a Faith Event

I do not want to speak here about the relationship of faith and the eucharist in general terms but only of the use of the time of receiving the communion as a distinct point in which one is enabled to accept Jesus as personal Savior and Lord. *The Book of Common Prayer*, in the context of the services of Holy Baptism and confirmation, does not hesitate to provide clear models for the public witness to the acceptance of Jesus as Savior and Lord. Even though conversion is a process, it has many turning points along the way, and those turning points are a necessary part of the process. The question often confronting us in the evangelization of nominal Christians is "What kind of opportunities for turning can we provide?" The model provided by evangelical Protestant Christianity, that of the altar call and the long walk down the aisle for a personal prayer of confession and the acceptance of Jesus, is occasionally useful within the Episcopal congregation at special events, such as a Faith Alive conference. For most Episcopalians most of the time, such a method utilized in a Sunday morning worship service would be like wearing one brown shoe and one black shoe to church. As effective as the ordinary altar call is in some settings, it does not fit well with our sense of liturgy. Nevertheless, it is necessary to provide that opportunity for turning, even on a Sunday morning during a eucharist. As Michael Green has pointed out, the apostolic Church was interested in results.

> The apostles were not shy about asking men to decide for or against the God who had decided for them. They expected results. They challenged men to do something about the message they had heard. The answer is clear enough in the pages of the New Testament. Men must do three things. They must repent, . . . Together with repentance comes faith; . . . The third condition . . . was, of course, baptism.[38]

We deal now with a problem that the early Church did not have, that of baptized people who have not yet come to faith. In the New Testament, baptism was readily available as an act of repentance and faith. Now baptism and its reaffirmation in confirmation involve waiting periods that did not hamper those who responded to the message of the apostles.

One way around that problem is to provide an easily available point of turning that can be used on any given time of eucharistic worship. We already have a built-in altar call. Every Episcopalian has the opportunity of going forward every Sunday to receive communion during eucharist. We have already seen in this chapter that the time of receiving communion can also become a time of receiving the laying on of hands and prayers for healing. It is but a small step to extend that same model to provide an opportunity for each individual to accept Jesus in a public but dignified way that fits in with the natural flow of liturgical worship. All that is necessary is to extend the same type of invitation that is used above in a way adapted for the acceptance of Jesus as Savior and Lord. On those occasions when the context of the service and the sermon suggest that it is appropriate, the celebrant can add an additional instruction to the instructions on healing, saying, "If you would like to accept Jesus as your personal Savior and Lord, please raise your right hand just before you receive communion. When I ask what you would like prayer for, just tell me that you would like to accept Jesus. I will then lead you in a small prayer that I will ask you to repeat after me."

The Reverend Canon Dennis Bennett, a leader in renewal in the Episcopal Church, summarizes the immediate steps to conversion in the following passage and gives a model of the type of prayer that can be used informally at the altar rail. The model and the prayer only contemporize what is, after all, the teaching both of Scripture and *The Book of Common Prayer.*

How do you accept forgiveness and receive this new life?
1. Realize you've been lost and going in the wrong direction, and be willing to go God's way.
2. Admit that you've been wrong, and ask the Father to take away your guilt and sin by the Blood of Jesus.
3. Ask Jesus Christ, God's only begotten Son, to come into your life, and become your Savior and Lord (Rev. 3:20).
4. Believe He has come the minute you ask Him to. Thank Him for saving you and giving you the new life (I John 5:11–15).
Here is a simple prayer you might say if you have decided to receive Jesus.
"Dear Father, I believe that Jesus Christ is Your only begotten Son, and that He became a Human Being, shed His Blood and died on the Cross to clean away my guilt and sin that was separating me from You. I believe that he rose from the dead, physically, to give me new life. Lord Jesus, I invite you to come into my heart, I accept You as my Savior and Lord. I confess my sins, and ask You to wash

them away. I believe that You have come and are living in me right now. Thank You, Jesus!"[39]

While that type of prayer may seem more emotional than a prescripted liturgical statement, it does have the advantage of personalizing the faith event in a way that sometimes liturgy, by virtue of its very familiarity and formality, does not. Whether the celebrant uses the prayer above in such a setting or is comfortable in extemporizing that type of prayer is immaterial. What is important is that the prayer be presented in simple personalized language that the other person can identify with and follow easily. Personal pastoral contact with the individual after the decision has been made is recommended wherever possible and nothing should be taken for granted. No matter how many years church members have been sitting in the congregation, the pastor or priest may well discover that they, in fact, don't know how to pray, sometimes don't understand simple moral issues, and do not even own a Bible in readable modern English. Part of the follow-up procedure should be to make sure that the individual is in contact with others in the congregation who have already made a faith decision and that efforts are made to incorporate the individual in existing small groups or Bible studies. It is important that the individual know and learn to trust the pastor's continuing interest in them through a number of informal contacts in which one takes time to speak to the issues of faith, as well as in preplanned appointments. In addition to the ministry of the clergy, every Christian within the congregation has a role to play in respect to the marvelous advice of "The Didache": "Every day you should seek the company of saints to enjoy their refreshing conversation."[40]

Notes

1. *The Book of Common Prayer*, 13.

2. Ibid., 354.

3. H.M.D. Westin, "Renewal as Seen from Within a Traditional Catholic Spirituality," in *Open to the Spirit*, 72.

4. Ibid., 73.

5. A.M. Allchin, "Walking in the Spirit: Freedom and Tradition in the Church's Life," in *Open to the Spirit*, 159.

6. Ibid.

7. George MacDonald, *MacDonald*, 77.

8. Johnson and Malony, *Christian Conversion*, 109.

9. Matt. 26:26–29; Mark 14:22–25; Luke 22:17–20.

10. 1 Cor. 11:23–25.

11. *The Book of Common Prayer*, 363.

12. *Dictionary of New Testament Theology*, Vol. 3 (or S.V. Sōzo) 211–12.

13. Sarapion, *Bishop Sarapion's Prayer Book*, ed. John Wordsworth (Hamden, CT: Archon, 1964), 63.

14. *Dictionary of New Testament Theology*, Vol. 3 (or S.V. Sōzo) 212.

15. Sarapion, *Sarapion's Prayer Book*, 93.

16. Ibid.

17. Hippolytus, *Hippolytus*, 36.

18. "The Wisdom of Jesus the Son of Sirach", in John Wimber with Kevin Springer, *Power Healing* (San Francisco: Harper & Row, 1987), 140.

19. Wimber, *Power Healing*, 140.

20. Ibid., 174.

21. Ibid., 175.

22. Pierre Teilhard de Chardin, *Sur l'Amour* (Tours: l'Imprimerie Mame à Tours, 1967), 7.

23. Agnes Sanford, *The Healing Light* (St. Paul, MN: Macalester Park, 1949), 35.

24. Donovan, *Christianity Rediscovered*, 125.

25. Rom. 12:1, RSV.

26. Heb. 4:12–13, RSV.

27. Morton Kelsey, *Healing and Christianity* (New York: Harper & Row, 1973).

28. Emily Gardiner Neal, *The Healing Power of Christ* (New York: Hawthorn Books, 1972).

29. Francis MacNutt, *Healing* (Notre Dame: Ave Maria, 1977).

30. *The Book of Common Prayer*, 531.

31. Ibid., 453–61.

32. Ibid., 558–65.

33. Ibid., 561.

34. Wimber, *Power Healing*, 169.

35. Ibid., 142.

36. Ibid., 144.

37. Ibid., 42.

38. Green, *Evangelism in the Early Church*, 151–52.

39. Dennis and Rita Bennett, *The Holy Spirit and You* (Plainfield, NJ: Logos International, 1971), 14–15.

40. "The Didache," in *Early Christian Fathers*, ed. Cyril Richardson, Library of Christian Classics (Philadelphia: Westminster Press, 1953), 173.

6. Pastoral Interaction as an Effective Means of Evangelism

Pastoral Interaction as an Evangelically Significant Event

The model of a eucharistically centered approach to evangelism could be misconstrued as priestocentric because it is centered on the ministry given at the altar rail. Yet in the Episcopal Church not all the eucharistic functionaries are ordained to a priestly or a diaconal ministry, as the cup is now very commonly ministered by licensed chalice bearers. There is, in fact, no reason why lay-people could not actually administer the prayers for healing or for the acceptance of Jesus as Savior and Lord. Their doing so is purely a matter of the developing ministries of the congregation and their willingness to take a share in those ministries, according to their gifts. In *Encounter*, a paper reprinted in *Theological Foundations for Ministry* from the Fourth World Conference on Faith and Order, a common misconception of ministry is indicated and corrected:

> Ministers of the church are wrongly set *above* the people. To lead, to have the oversight and therefore to exhort, does indeed belong to their genuine functions, as will be shown later. But this never means to "lord over" or to set the pattern. It is significant that the New Testament writers never created and used the term "*hypertage.*" On the contrary, they introduced the term "*hypotage*," mutual submission.[1]

While the priest obviously functions within the congregation as a pastor, the pastoral gifts given by the Spirit, along with the gift of evangelism, are not confined to the priest who may, or may not, be as good in these areas as some members of his own congregation.

The priest is, after all, a member of the community, and it is within the community that the priest, the faithful believers, and the unbelievers and/or nominal Christians make their home. The community is a kenotic community whose nature is determined by the meaning of the dogma of *kenosis* and the self-emptying love it declares. This understanding of kenosis applied to the community is not a new static ethic to be lived by nor a new way of renunciation. It is nothing other than an indication of the participation of the community in the love of God understood from the perspective of the Incarnation. Of this, Ray S. Anderson says,

95

If we were to express the fundamental meaning of *kenosis*, then, it could be said to be the intrinsic character of divine love itself, and thus conceived as an activity rather than as an essence. The intrinsic character of this love has its clearest explication in the life of the Incarnate Logos, but this also clarifies the nature of man as created in the image of God. The dogma of *kenosis* tells us that the transcendence of God is as real in the image of God as for God himself. *Kenosis* can be, therefore, another way of understanding the image of God, or of stating the true nature of man. *Kenosis* means that man has his true nature completed when he participates in the intra-divine transcendence (love), and that this participation does not involve the repudiation or violation of that which is truly human.[2]

One of the effects of viewing the community kenotically is that the relationship of priest and people can no longer be understood with an authoritarian hierarchical model. All within the community are called to self-emptying, to a receiving of one another, and to an extension of personal support for one another that sounds suspiciously Pauline.

So if there is any encouragement in Christ, any incentive of love, any participation in the Spirit, any affection and sympathy, complete my joy by being of the same mind, having the same love, being in full accord and of one mind. Do nothing from selfishness or conceit, but in humility count others better than yourselves. Let each of you look not only to his own interests, but also to the interests of others.[3]

That is, of course, by the obvious context of the above passage, exactly the application that Paul gives to the dogma of *kenosis*, which is not stated as an abstract concept but in relation to the functioning of the Christian community. The community itself is part of God's self-revelation to the world. Regarding the community, Ray S. Anderson says,

There are two marks of visibility for the transcendence of God at this point. One is the visibility of historical transcendence in the revelation concerning God's act in Jesus Christ as contained in the Scriptures. This is a form of visibility which assumes an audible form as the Word of God is "heard," and yet, one is ultimately confronted by the historical existence of the Word as Jesus Christ. The other form of visibility is the presence of the Spirit in the concrete life of the other person in the community, or, one could say, in the concrete existence of the community itself.[4]

I assume that the unbeliever, and/or the nominal Christian, is already within the congregation. Indeed, in the case of nominal

Christians it is not always easy to identify that their faith is, in fact, nominal. Nevertheless, the community in which they dwell is a community of fellowship with the Father and with our Lord Jesus Christ. The community is a place where the individual encounters others who share a living faith. By the grace and action of the Holy Spirit that transcendence becomes visible kenotically in the real lives of men and women as they suffer, fail, and sometimes share victories in the presence of Jesus. These encounters form the first and most significant pastoral interaction, from which all other pastoral interactions flow.

> It is at this point, however, that the one who is "received" in this kenotic way is touched at the crucial point of his own "receptivity." To receive the Spirit of God in this way, represents a radical and devastating confrontation with one's actual situation of spiritual autonomy, which we have already called estrangement from fellowship with God. To receive now means a reversal of the Ego and a "turning towards" the transcendence of God with openness and a "change of mind" *(metanoia)* which represents a conversion to God in the deepest sense of the word.[5]

One thing that ought to be apparent is that this kind of "devastating confrontation," by its very nature, will cause stress to the individual in the process of undergoing it and that the individual may transfer that distress to the community at large. This takes place, not in an abstract idealized community, but in the kenotic community as it, in fact, is.

> It seems clear from the character of kenotic community as it has been exposed, that a conversion "experience" cannot be demanded as the qualifying act on the part of a person for his belonging to the kenotic community. This has some very important implications.[6]

One of those implications has already been seen in relationship to the healing ministry at the altar rail. Participation within the body of Christ cannot neatly be confined only to those who have faith, over against those whose measure of faith is dubious. The eucharist is open to all baptized Christians, nominal or not!

> But it must also immediately be said that participation in the kenotic community does involve receiving as well as being received. And it may well be that only after "being received" for a considerable length of love (one would naturally say "time," but those "lengths" have a duration which only love can measure!) can a person muster the strength and the will to receive. This is, of course, what is entailed in the second aspect of the character of the kenotic community; it

offers to each person, to the extent that he is able to bear it, an *actual* growth into the reality of his own personhood, which is the capacity to live in love.[7]

Evident here is the absolute necessity, not only of the living witness within the community but of calm patience as the word that is given by the living witness begins to mature. That period of maturation may be, in the words of Anderson, "a considerable length of love." The end goal of conversion is Christian maturity, or the evolvement of personhood. "The kenotic community can be said then to be the 'home of personhood' where a man is both received as a person and then, at the same time, receives his personhood."[8] Providing that context is the function of all the members of the Body of Christ, priest and people alike. That function is the full meaning of pastoral interaction.

That seems like an impossibly challenging task for the community of believers including its priest, but we are not really talking of ideals and nonexistent perfection. The Church is as you see it: often beleaguered and beset from within and without. It is at once a *communio sanctorum* and a *communio peccatorum*.

> Yet the community of earth, the *communio sanctorum*, lives in the persons of these many Christians who are so terribly assailed and harassed; of the *sancti* who both as a whole and as individuals are also *peccatores*, and in whom the spirit may be willing enough but the flesh is weak. The *communio* itself is assailed as they are assailed. It can grow only as there takes place the *communio* of these members in relation both to the *sancta* and to one another.[9]

The witness is carried out in the midst of an imperfect kenotic community, hence the strong note of humiliation in the kenosis of the Christ. Only a witness that springs from the reality of one's life has the hope of touching other sinful men and women where they are and bringing them into the light of a transcendent God. A witness that professes a sinless perfection has by that profession distanced itself from its own reality and the reality of others. Pastoral interaction is not a reaching from above, but a standing beside that is only possible when those who are doing the reaching have accepted the implications of their own humanity under grace.

How weak is the kenotic community?

> It is one thing to say that the kenotic community is formed of actual people, it is quite another thing to know how actually sick, how actually weak, how actually unable to love, and how actually unlovable actual people can be! But here is where the kenotic community

establishes its real character, for it dares to include those who have the capacity (and often the compulsion) to destroy the community itself, and even more, it dares to offer love as a possibility of growth. The same Spirit who led Jesus to choose Judas as one of his intimate followers prior to the resurrection, baptized Ananias and Sapphira into the kenotic community of lived transcendence. Here we see that the true kenotic community is marked, not by whom it is willing to renounce, but whom it is willing to receive. But there is more implied in this "receiving" than a blind spot at the center of one's vision. For the "being received" is a participation in lived transcendence, for such is the nature of kenotic community.[10]

It is not as though only a few were afflicted with the weaknesses of humanity. All are! Pastoral interaction is carried out between real human beings with all the limitations and potentials for failure and for marvelous success through grace that that implies. It is also evident that the necessary character of a kenotic community lays itself open for serious failure. That failure, however, is the way of the cross; it is the extent to which *kenosis* was carried out by the Christ. So Paul says poignantly of his own ministry, "Now I rejoice in my sufferings for your sake, and in my flesh I complete what is lacking in Christ's sufferings for the sake of his body, that is, the church, . . ."[11]

Pastoral interaction, as a deliberative ministry of the Body of Christ is preferably carried by the more gifted in terms of counseling, encouragement, and special offers of support. The ordained clergy may—perhaps in some settings even ought to—be at the center of that work, but he may not be the most skilled. That ministry in the midst of the Church as we find it today is one that cannot be carried out by an isolated individual but one that cries out to be shared with others in the Body of Christ. That work of extending health to one another for the sake of Christ is not, however, the exclusive property of a gifted few but is the call of every Christian for every other.

The Sacramental Act of the Reconciliation of a Penitent

It is one of the strengths of the new Prayer Book that the reconciliation of penitents is not rigidly confined to the priesthood. This reconciliation is a natural function and result of pastoral interaction kenotically understood. Of it, the Prayer Book says,

The ministry of reconciliation, which has been committed by Christ to his Church, is exercised through the care each Christian has for others, through the common prayer of Christians assembled for public worship, and through the priesthood of the Church and its ministers declaring absolution. . . . Confessions may be heard anytime and anywhere. . . . Another Christian may be asked to hear a confession, but it must be made clear to the penitent that absolution will not be pronounced; instead, a declaration of forgiveness is provided. . . . The secrecy of a confession is morally absolute for the confessor, and must under no circumstances be broken.[12]

"The Reconciliation of a Penitent," as a liturgical framework for repentance, is a normal way for leading the new penitent, or any other penitent, back to the Father. Such a reconciliation invokes the grace of God for a restoration of the baptismal state.

Holy God, heavenly Father, you formed me from the dust in your image and likeness, and redeemed me from sin and death by the cross of your Son Jesus Christ. Through the water of baptism you clothed me with the shining garment of his righteousness, and established me among your children in your kingdom. But I have squandered the inheritance of your saints, and have wandered in a land that is waste. . . . I turn to you in sorrow and repentance. Receive me again into the arms of your mercy, and restore me to the blessed company of your faithful people; through him in whom you have redeemed the world, your Son our Savior Jesus Christ. Amen.[13]

Whether intentional or not, the theology of the restoration of the penitent, even by virtue of the very term *restoration*, is consonant with the understanding of conversion within the context of a covenant community whose members alike without exception have been baptized, generally as infants, and most often stand in the position of having to reawaken the power of that sacrament by a conscious act of repentance and the acceptance of Jesus as Savior and Lord. The acceptance of Jesus as Savior and Lord is not repeated at this place in the prayer book "reawakening" of the meaning of baptism, and it is left to the individual who is making his or her confession, and to the person hearing that confession in the presence of God, to make the acceptance of Jesus specific and conscious through a simple prayer of surrender to Jesus as Savior and Lord, or the renewal of the same, at the time of formal reassurance of God's forgiveness. There is, indeed, no sense in making a confession without the intention of amendment of life in the personal following of Jesus as Savior and Lord.

Because the reconciliation of a penitent is a natural function and result of a kenotic understanding of pastoral interaction, care must be taken that those who are called to lead others to him in this way are themselves prepared for this ministry. They need to understand that "the true kenotic community is marked, not by whom it is willing to renounce, but whom it is willing to receive."[14] Those who seek to receive others so that they may receive Christ must develop a capacity for what Henri J.M. Nouwen calls "hospitality":

> Hospitality is the virtue which allows us to break through the narrowness of our own fears and to open our houses to the stranger, with the intuition that salvation comes to us in the form of a tired traveller. Hospitality makes anxious disciples into powerful witnesses, . . .[15]

In referring to "our houses" Nouwen is really referring to the personal space that is an aspect of our personhood, that is, we open *ourselves* to the other. It is not only the "narrowness of our own fears" that we must deal with but those other elements of human frailty that are so often the subject of personal confession. We must become comfortable with ourselves, as we are, before we are truly able to be open to receive others.

> What does hospitality as a healing power require? It requires first of all that the host feel at home in his own house, and secondly that he create a free and fearless place for the unexpected visitor.[16]

Those who come to us in the midst of the community, including those hiding behind the mask of nominalism, come fraught with self-doubt and suffering the pains of alienation—alienation from God, from humankind, and even from themselves. The very hiddeness of nominalism declares, "I am afraid that if I allow myself to be truly seen, I will prove to be unacceptable." Unless we ourselves live as reconciled beings, we will not be able to communicate God's acceptance to others.

> But how can we avoid this danger? I think by no other way than to enter ourselves first of all into the center of our existence and become familiar with the complexities of our inner lives. As soon as we feel at home in our own house, discover the dark corners as well as the light spots, the closed doors as well as the drafty rooms, our confusion will evaporate, our anxiety will diminish, and we will become capable of creative work.
>   The key word here is articulation. . . .This articulation, I believe, is the basis for a spiritual leadership of the future, because only he who is able to articulate his own experience can offer himself to others as a source of clarification.[17]

This articulation must by necessity take several forms, among them, verbalized sharing of one's own spiritual journey in both formal and informal settings. Part of the very witness of the kenotic community lies in the ability of some of its members to share both their moments of personal humiliation and the work of grace that brought them through. While it is not customary within the patterns of Episcopal worship to make a time for the giving of personal witness, there is no reason other than unfounded custom for not doing so. Many Episcopal churches have a custom of providing a children's talk within "The Word of God" during Holy Eucharist. This occurs at various times, such as between lections, in lieu of a sermon, or even during the announcement period. There is no reason why time cannot be allowed similarly for the giving of personal witness. Yet that is not the only forum for witness. Sometimes the most effective personal witness to one's own humiliation and reconciliation is given informally over a cup of coffee.

The validity of the witness is apt to be measured, rightly, by the depth and reality of one's sharing and by how well one has bound one's own wounds.

> Making one's own wounds a source of healing, therefore, does not call for a sharing of superficial personal pains but for a constant willingness to see one's own pain and suffering as rising from the depth of the human condition which all men share.[18]

It is that understanding of the connection of one's own reality with the reality of others that is the touchstone of a kenotic approach to pastoral interaction and to the reconciliation of penitents.

How well one binds one's own wounds is part of the measure by which the validity of one's witness to grace in the midst of the community will be understood.

> So it is too with the minister. Since it is his task to make visible the first vestiges of liberation for others, he must bind his own wounds carefully in anticipation of the moment when he will be needed. He is called to be the wounded healer, the one who must look after his own wounds but at the same time be prepared to heal the wounds of others.[19]

Nouwen is speaking here primarily of the minister as "Christian leader, minister, or priest."[20] But I want to take care to expand it to include anyone who ministers within the context of an informed and deliberate pastoral interaction with the intention of leading another person to Christ.

> In this context pastoral conversation is not merely a skillful use of conversational techniques to manipulate people into the Kingdom of God, but a deep human encounter in which a man is willing to put his own faith and doubt, his own hope and despair, his own

light and darkness at the disposal of others who want to find a way through their confusion and touch the solid core of life.[21]

That is the central focus of pastoral interaction as it fulfills a dynamic role within the kenotic community as those who have found the way share that way with others and bring them into reconciliation with God.

Baptism and Confirmation in Relation to the Empowering of the Holy Spirit

Now is the time to go back once again to the covenant understanding of baptism and confirmation. The former is an act of faith of the covenant community, which as a kenotic community is emphatically interested in the inclusion of its children, and the latter is a reaffirmation of that covenant faith by the person now come of age. For them the postbaptismal prayer is potentially realized.

> Heavenly Father, we thank you that by water and the Holy Spirit you have bestowed upon *these* your *servants* the forgiveness of sin, and have raised *them* to the new life of grace. Sustain *them*, O Lord, in your Holy Spirit. Give *them* an inquiring and discerning heart, the courage to will and to persevere, a spirit to know and to love you, and the gift of joy and wonder in all your works.[22]

The forgiveness of sin is not to be thought of as merely propositional but as something experientially possessed, as is also the new life of grace. While these things are, in fact, possessed and experienced, we are not to think of ourselves as having arrived so much as being on the way. The balance of the prayer speaks to the process of being on the way as it asks God to sustain the believer and give the "courage to will and to persevere." This is indeed what we had seen in Hans Küng in our earlier discussion on the awakening of baptism.

> *Baptism*, at first received only passively by the child, now becomes effective as a result of the young person's actively grasping the offer of grace with explicit faith, with the profession of faith and with action in the light of faith.
> The *Spirit*, granted at baptism as effective power, now becomes an existential reality, determining the young person's faith and life.[23]

Again, that is to say that confirmation not only looks backward to baptism, but it also looks to the future and the ministry of the individual who is now strengthened and empowered by the Holy Spirit for service in the Body of Christ.

It is important to restate at this time that baptism and its reaffirmation in confirmation is, in effect, a time of lay ordination at the hands of the bishop who prays, "Send *them* forth in the power of that Spirit to perform the service you set before *them*," and then lays his hands on each believer.[24] These prayers again are not without an experiential side for the believer who, through his baptism and the laying on of the bishop's hands, receives by faith the gifts of the Spirit inherent in his baptism. Baptism and confirmation are the ordination of the laity as through their receptive faith *charisms*, or gifts of the Spirit, are imparted for ministry.

But what is the nature of these charisms?

> On the basis of all the foregoing evidence we can attempt a theological description of what charism means; in its widest sense it signifies *the call of God, addressed to an individual, to a particular ministry in the community, which brings with it the ability to fulfil that ministry*. We have seen how interconnected charism, vocation and service are; terminologically they seem to merge together; thus "charisms" can alternate with "services" (I Cor. 12:4-6) or with "vocation" (Rom. 11:29; I Cor. 7:7). Prerequisites for "services" are "charisms" and "vocation."
>
> Taking charism in this widest sense, rather than seeing it as a strange, exceptional and miraculous power, we can translate the word simply as "gift of grace" (in secular language there is often an overlap between the ideas of a "gift" for something and a "vocation" for something). But charisms are expressions of God's grace and power, in the Spirit. They all point to the one great charism of God, the new life which has been given to us in Christ Jesus; "The charism of God is eternal life in Christ Jesus our Lord" (Rom. 6:23; cf. Rom. 5:15f.).[25]

That is, the ministry of the kenotic community is charismatic in its basic nature and that charismatic quality cannot be confined to the charisms most commonly identified in lists of the gifts of the Spirit, nor does it exclude them. Rather the charisms of individual members of the community exist for the service of the community and the world, and that service, in the form of Christian vocation, calls forth the charisms from the gift-giving Spirit in the experience of everyday men and women. While the charisms are implicit in the baptism and confirmation of each individual, they are not at all limited to what the individual immediately experiences but remain there, dormant as it were, awaiting the task that will call them into active being. From this perspective,

> charism is no longer extraordinary or unexpected but is the common rule for the structure of the community. For Paul charism means

simply the concrete function that each person exercises within the community for the good of all (cf. I Cor 12:7; Rom 12:4; Eph 4:7). Paul details this model by stating that the Church is a body with many members, all springing from the Spirit itself, each with its unique function. There is no uncharismatic member, no one is useless, everyone occupies a decisive place in the community: "each member serves the other members" (Rom 12:5).[26]

Among the charisms within the Body of Christ are the charisms of evangelism and those charisms that make the pastoral interaction of some members of the kenotic community savingly powerful above that of other members of the community whose charisms will lead them to place more emphasis in serving in other areas. From this point of view, "baptism is the ordination into the apostolic, charismatic and sacrificial ministry of the church"[27] so that the church cannot remain a consumer church but must become apostolic and thus missionary.[28]

The result is that preparatory counseling and teaching that precedes baptism and confirmation must be undertaken with deliberate clarity about the nature of baptism and confirmation as, not just an incorporation into membership, but as an equipping for service. Those who are thus prepared are made ready to receive the person of Jesus and the charisms that he inevitably brings with him. Within that context of the preparation for a right receiving or reawakening of baptism and confirmation, it is necessary that those who would counsel, teach, and lead others into the fullness of the faith must themselves be those for whom that same faith has become alive, rather than merely propositional.

Pastoral Visitation and the Discovery of Faith

Some theological education in the late 1960s advocated pastoral visitation in hospitals and homes but surprisingly conveyed no adequate reason why these aspects of the ministry of the Church should be undertaken. The assumption was, in the case of hospitals, that one went to comfort and, in the homes, one went to establish human contact with the congregation. Underlying those assumptions was the tacit understanding that it was the minister or priest who made the call, and that somehow he or she was the content of the call. This has been so dominant an understanding that in many congregations where there are multiple clergy, members do not feel that they have received a pastoral visit unless it is the rector who has called. Somehow even the ordained assistant doesn't qualify as an adequate pastoral caller. That assumption is an ongoing frustration for a number of team ministries.

As is the case in the leadership of prayers at the altar rail, there is no theological reason why members of the congregation should not themselves fulfill this ministry even to the point of bearing the major burden in these areas. For this to happen, not only do the charisms and resulting ministries of others in the Body of Christ need to be raised up, but considerable education through preaching, teaching, and supervised practice of various ministries needs to be systematically carried out. But even the design and implementation of these types of programs need to be a shared ministry and an example itself of the unfolding of the gifts of the laity. The type of leadership called for by these actual needs for the unfolding of the gifts of the members of the Body of Christ cannot be carried out at a distance.

> By speaking about articulation as a form of leadership we have already suggested the place where the future leader will stand. Not "up there," far away or secretly hidden, but in the midst of his people with the utmost visibility.[29]

The pastoral leader does indeed need to be in the midst of the people, present with them in their sorrows and triumphs, but sharing also with them that very ministry itself. The ministry of visitation is a kenotic ministry that "offers to each person, to the extent that he is able to bear it, an actual growth into the reality of his own personhood, which is the capacity to live in love."[30] Whether the call is in the hospital with the offer of comfort, counsel, and prayers for healing or in the home, the actual content of the call is Jesus Christ himself. What makes the call "pastoral" is the presence and reality of the Spirit of Jesus within the human encounter.

> This reality of the Spirit cannot be called the historical transcendence of God, for that belongs uniquely to the life of the Incarnate Word, but should rather be called a lived transcendence by which the reality of God impinges upon the world through the historical existence of the man who lives in the Spirit of God.[31]

The offer of personhood is one that can ultimately be made in Christ. The promise and potentiality of that personhood is sacramentally embraced in the reaffirmation of our baptism in confirmation. Of this, the late medieval mystic Jan Van Ruysbroeck said,

You should know that all spirits in their return toward God receive names; each one in particular, according to the nobleness of its service and the loftiness of its love. For only the first name of innocence, which we receive at baptism is adorned with the merits of our Lord Jesus Christ. And when we have lost this name of innocence through sin, if we are still willing to follow God—we are baptized once more in the Holy Ghost. And thereby we receive a new name which shall remain with us throughout eternity.[32]

In Van Ruysbroeck, this new name is seen in the sparkling stone that one holds in the palm of one's hand,[33] and that sparkling stone is our Lord Jesus Christ.[34] To carry out that ministry of calling forth the identity of others in Christ, one must, like Christ in his *kenosis*, step across the barriers and antipathies that divide human beings from each other. "For the compassionate man nothing is alien: no joy and no sorrow, no way of living and no way of dying."[35] To be involved in this type of pastoral interaction requires a charism of courage and humility that must extend far beyond places of personal safety.

> . . . it seems necessary to re-establish the basic principle that no one can help anyone without becoming involved, without entering with his whole person into the painful situation, without taking the risk of becoming hurt, wounded or even destroyed in the process. The beginning and the end of all Christian leadership is to give your life for others. Thinking about martyrdom can be an escape unless we realize that real martyrdom means a witness that starts with the willingness to cry with those who cry, laugh with those who laugh, and to make one's own painful and joyful experiences available as sources of clarification and understanding.[36]

At all times, whether in the hospital where it may be of immediate eternal significance or in the home, one ought to stand ready to call the other into personal faith and lead them in the acceptance of Jesus as Savior and Lord. For if Jesus is the ultimate content of pastoral visitation he must be finally given with such reasonableness and compassion, and with such dignity and simplicity, that he can be, indeed, received and known by those who stand in need of him.

Notes

1. Fourth World Conference on Faith and Order, "Christ's Ministry Through His Whole Church," in *Theological Foundations for Ministry*, 437.

2. Ray S. Anderson, "Living in the Spirit", in *Theological Foundations for Ministry*, 309.

3. Phil. 2:1–4, RSV.

4. Anderson, "Living in the Spirit," 312.

5. Ibid.

6. Ibid., 312–13.

7. Ibid., 313.

8. Ibid.

9. Karl Barth, "The Growth of the Community," in *Theological Foundations for Ministry*, 287.

10. Anderson, "Living in the Spirit," 311.

11. Col. 1:24, RSV.

12. *The Book of Common Prayer*, 446.

13. Ibid., 450.

14. Anderson, "Living in the Spirit," 311.

15. Henri J.M. Nouwen, *The Wounded Healer* (Garden City: Image, 1979), 89.

16. Ibid.

17. Ibid., 38.

18. Ibid., 88.

19. Ibid., 82.

20. Ibid., 39.

21. Ibid.

22. *The Book of Common Prayer*, 308.

23. Küng, *Signposts*, 196.

24. *The Book of Common Prayer*, 418.

25. Hans Küng, "The Continuing Charismatic Structure," in *Theological Foundations for Ministry*, 486–87.

26. Leonardo Boff, *Church: Charism & Power* (New York: Crossroad, 1986), 157.

27. Fourth World Conference on Faith and Order, "Christ's Ministry," 434.

28. Ibid., 443.

29. Nouwen, *Wounded Healer*, 400.

30. Anderson, "Living in the Spirit," 311.

31. Ibid., 304.

32. Jan Van Ruysbroeck, "The Sparkling Stone," in *Late Medieval Mysticism*, Library of Christian Classics (Philadelphia: Westminster Press, 1957), 298.

33. Rev. 2:17b, RSV.

34. Jan Van Ruysbroeck, "The Sparkling Stone," in *Late Medieval Mysticism*, edited by Ray C. Petry. Library of Christian Classics (Philadelphia: Westminster Press, 1957), 297.

35. Nouwen, *Wounded Healer*, 41.

36. Ibid., 72.

7. An Approach to Conflicts Generated by the Proclamation of the Gospel

The Resistance or Receptivity of Various Groups within the Parish

In the introduction I noted that the Sunday morning congregation includes a wide variety of people, from the barely conscious worshiper who seems to be fulfilling some vaguely perceived obligation to be there to the radical enthusiast of "being there" who may or may not have any desire to be touched on deeper levels. Within that span are those who have already made a conscious decision to accept Jesus as Savior, without having a realistic perception of the call to the lordship of Christ, and those who rejoice in the saving work of Jesus and are, in fact, trying to work out the meaning of his lordship in practical terms within their own lives. As the process of evangelization moves forward within the parish environment, lives do begin to change, for better and for worse, and with the change of lives there is an accompanying change in the dynamics and power structures of the parish. It is often a distressing discovery to find power groupings within a Christian community. But the Kingdom of God is not truly incarnate in human community unless it is also incarnate in a logical fashion within its power structures.

To a great extent the changing dynamics are a direct result of the nature of conversion itself. In discussing the Old Testament word for "turning to or from, turning away, *or* returning, or 'conversion,' "[1] Johnson and Malony point out that

> as it is used in the Old Testament, *shubh* has a twofold stress. It means a reversal *from* something and a turning to something else. The person who is converted leaves one context and way of life and turns to another—to God, His people, and the way of life prescribed by Him.[2]

If that twofold turning were to happen in a vacuum, everything would be very simple. But the truth is that it happens in the midst of a community comprised of a wide variety of people, not all of whom have come to the Church for the correct reasons. Dietrich Bonhoeffer brings the reality into sharp focus:

111

> The old world cannot take pleasure in the Church because the Church speaks of its end as though it had already happened—as though the world had already been judged. The old world does not like being regarded as dead. The Church has never been surprised at this, nor is it surprised by the fact that again and again men come to it who think the thoughts of the old world—and who is there entirely free from them? But the Church is naturally in tumult when these children of the world that has passed away lay claim to the Church, to the new, for themselves. They want the new and only know the old. And thus they deny Christ the Lord.[3]

In a sense the presence of the children of the world within the Church is a cause for rejoicing. The work of the Church, after all, is bringing those who do not yet believe into the Kingdom of God. On the other hand, a strong numerical imbalance between converted and unconverted people can create difficulty for the process of evangelization within the congregation, especially when those who have not been converted control the individual congregation.

Some of the insights of Donald McGavran on the nature of church growth in relationship to missions is helpful when applied to the individual congregation. While, in a sense, each parish is more or less a homogeneous unit, within each parish, no matter how homogeneous, there are, in fact, subgroups roughly analogous to McGavran's groupings for mission areas. These subgroups are very homogeneous within themselves even though they may belong to a larger homogeneous unit. Reading McGavran in the light of this is very helpful:[4]

> To what degree is becoming a Christian a real option to members of this homogeneous unit? How receptive is it? In answering these questions or estimating the receptivity of any population it is helpful to locate it on a receptivity axis of distribution. If a line is drawn, such as that in the following figure from A to Z, every population can be located at the letter which corresponds to its likelihood to become Christian. At A would be placed those peoples who solidly resist Christianity. At Z would be those whose members break down all barriers in order to become Christian. In between, all other populations would be distributed according to their degree of responsiveness.

DISTRIBUTION OF RECEPTIVITY

A B C	J	S	X	Z

This axis along with another axis later in his book need to be placed together before drawing a similar axis based on the congregation.[5]

At the left end of the axis would be grouped tight, closed societies, powerful and satisfied peoples, and well-disciplined tribes with high people-consciousness. The more political and military power a people has, the closer to the left end of the line it would be placed.

1	2	3	4	5	6	7	8	9	10

Tight, closed,	Loose, open, weak,
powerful, satisfied,	dissatisfied,
well-disciplined,	ill-disciplined,
proud peoples	humble peoples

To apply this to a parish setting, a primary descriptive phrase needs to be changed: *military power*. The phrase that needs to be substituted is *financial power*. The largest giver may have this power, as is sometimes the case. But more likely, the power-holder controls the finances within the parish structure, whether or not he or she has money or even pledges. One of the most troublesome individuals I have experienced in the process of evangelism was a parish treasurer and finance chairperson who, in fact, did not give a regular pledge in a setting where there were several substantial tithers who remained outside of the actual power structures of the parish. The simple reason for the tithers' lack of status was they didn't have any to begin with, which was no doubt a contributing factor to their receptivity to the call to conversion. With the change to *financial power*, McGavran's description is an accurate one of the left end of the spectrum: "Tight, closed, powerful, satisfied, well-disciplined, proud peoples." The application of "tight, closed, powerful, satisfied, and proud" is easier to understand than "well-disciplined" in this context. However, the left-end subgroups within the parish, while perhaps containing undisciplined individuals, usually are well-disciplined in the sense that their subgroup is limited and controlled by fairly rigid mores that protect the group from intrusive elements. On the other hand, the right-end description is an apt one for those subgroups within the parish who are most susceptible to the gospel from the outset. They are the "loose, open, weak, dissatisfied, ill-disciplined, humble peoples." Lest that cause an immediate negative reaction, one needs to consider Jesus' view of his own ministry in the light of the social groupings of his day.

And Levi made him a great feast in his house; and there was a large company of tax collectors and others sitting at table with them; And the Pharisees and their scribes murmured against his disciples, saying, "Why do you eat and drink with tax collectors and sinners?" And Jesus answered them, "Those who are well have no need of a physician, but those who are sick; I have not come to call the righteous, but sinners to repentance."[6]

In table 1, the grouping also follows the pattern of McGavran's, with the most closed on the left and the most open on the right. The various groups are identified by capital letters whose meanings are clear from the list below and follow from left to right. The types identified are from my own observation. Above the line are four categories of outreach or ministry appropriate for different ranges on the axis.

Table 1. Outreach to Parish Subgroups

CHAPLAINCY	PROCLAMATION	PERSUASION	OPEN EVANGELISM
Presence, integrity, persistence, fortitude, parish politics	Same as on the left but with light evangelistic challenges	Special evangelism programs, Bible study, personal persuasion	Open appeals, strong challenges (methods under next column at left)

(L) (BN) (P) (H) (PB) (BD) (S) (SL) (FS)   (N) (YC)   (RH) (NS) (OL) (N1) (B)

CLOSED			OPEN
strongly	somewhat	neutral	somewhat	strongly

In the following list, expressions such as *lay popes* and *bleeding deacons* are descriptive colloquialisms drawn from various social groupings. Other names for subgroups are self-explanatory.

(L)   *Lay Popes* usually occur singly, or in a small college of cardinals, and treat the incumbent clergy like servants to be directed at their slightest whim. They usually are old, long-term members of the parish who are often substantial givers.

(BN) *Benefactors* are major givers and their family clusters who enjoy the power of being benefactors. If a parish is dominated by a large benefactor family cluster, or more than one, it may make evangelism within the parish extremely difficult.

(P)   *Pioneers* are founding members of a parish whose ownership is established by the process of founding the parish. This tends not to be operative in parishes that have been established fairly recently.

(H)   *Homesteaders* may not be founding members, but their long tenure has given an ownership just as firm.

(PB) *Power Board* members are usually a cluster of ruling people within the parish that stay together, often interchanging vestry positions with each other, or with their like-minded spouses, when their terms are up. They rule together whether they are in office or not.

(BD) *Bleeding Deacons* are holy whiners with a strong sense of ownership and too much identity wrapped into a function that they fill in the parish. In communicating this function and making demands on others they do so with uncomfortable intensity and frequently project guilt on others in their attempts to gain cooperation.

(S) *Storekeepers* mind the shop faithfully for the groups above and derive their identity from the approval of those whom they serve. This sometimes might include a parish secretary or organist or members of the finance committee or women's groups. Storekeepers have a strong sense of ownership but live in fear and dependency on those they serve.

(SL) *Social Lions* tend to belong to the parish for social reasons, which include their relationships with those above.

(FS) *Faithful Servants* are just like Storekeepers, but they have no real ownership and end up most of the time serving the Storekeepers.

(N) *New People* are very often drawn to a parish for a variety of reasons, not all of them consonant with the aims of the gospel. In a partially renewed parish some new people will not stay because of the preaching of the gospel, some will align themselves with the groups above, and a greater number will be positive and responsive, particularly if the initial contacts from the parish and clergy keep the gospel up front as a priority.

(YC) *Young Couples*, about to be married, newly married, or with young children, even though they may fit into family clusters in the above groups, are in life situations where there is frequent change, instability, and the stresses that come with new marriages or new families. Young couples as a result are often open to persuasion combined with pastoral care and to counseling for sacraments or sacramental acts, all of which can lead to faith decisions.

(RH) *Recent Homesteaders* are those who have not yet established ownership in the parish but nevertheless have been in the parish for some time before the clergy's arrival. Leave them alone long enough and they will become true homesteaders and, as a result, more resistant to evangelization.

(NS) *Non-Status* members usually include a fairly wide selection of people who often outnumber the groups on the left side of the line. For one reason or another they have not been admitted into the left-end groups and remain partially alienated from the parish although in regular attendance. Frequently, members of this group will be nominal in matters of faith, as will members of the other subgroups, but Non-Status members will often be very open to evangelism.

(OL) *Old Lonely* members, often on the shut-in list, are very frequently open to loving personal evangelism, especially when it is accompanied by genuine concern for their well-being and by prayers for healing.

(N1) *Needy* members are those whose needs are fairly evident and may even have some grasp of their own neediness. Note: It is possible for any member of any of the above subgroups to fall into this category at a time of crisis. Consistent pastoral care for all members of the parish is an important part of evangelism.

(B) *Believers* in the congregation, who have already made a conscious faith decision, are allies in prayer, planning, and actual evangelism.

The common thread that binds all these various subgroups and individuals together within the parish is that membership, no matter how it is conceived or how lightly it is held, is part of each person's identity. To be converted may be either to gain positive identity (that is, to be affirmed as a valuable and worthwhile individual), or to be converted may mean at first sight an apparent loss of status and identity in relation to one's subgroup. The relative size of each of the subgroups will give some insight into the possible success of evangelization within the parish.[7] A disproportionately large subgroup of benefactors will signal potential difficulty, while on the other hand, a parish that is numerically dominated by right-end subgroups will be more responsive to evangelization. A side problem that is raised by this comes at the time of considering a call to a new parish ministry. The left-end dominated parish may well look more successful in terms of organization, finance, and social activities and be very unresponsive to evangelization, while the right-end parish may be poorly organized and show a number of signs of low self-value yet be the better choice for evangelism and eventual church growth.

It is natural in the process of the evangelization of nominal Christians within the worshiping congregation to have two basic responses. The left-end response is described well by George MacDonald when he asks, "Can it be any comfort to them to be told that God loves them so that He will burn them clean? . . . They do not want to be clean, and they cannot bear to be tortured."[8] Strong left-end subgroups primarily want to be left alone, and often the way to appeal to members of those groups is to provide faithful chaplaincy services, especially at times of crisis and times of change in life situations that may open some individuals up to grace. Baptism, confirmation, marriage, burial, and other obvious points of contact must be used wisely and lovingly, yet not restrictively in order to reach these groups. A difficulty arises for them and perhaps for the process of evangelization in the normal course of the proclamation of the gospel. Not only do they not want to be told that God "will burn them clean"; they, like the Pharisees of old, emphatically do not want to discover that they are not clean already. At times they fear the very presence of God reflected in the faces and lives of others, and they fear what God may demand of them if they surrender to him.

> And is not God ready to do unto them even as they fear, though with another feeling and a different end from any which they are capable of supposing? He is against sin: insofar as, and while, they and sin are one, He is against them—against their desires, their aims, their fears, and their hopes; and thus He is altogether and always *for them*.[9]

The situation is well illustrated by a scene from a small parish that I was rector of a number of years ago. There had been a marvelous movement of the Holy Spirit in the right-end subgroups of the parish, and a number of needy people were drawn to the parish and converted. Their lives were joyfully and very evidently changed. One of the Power Board members was having a great deal of difficulty with the evidence of new life in some of these people. One day I asked him, "Al, what is it about these people that bothers you?" He looked at the ceiling, then down at his feet, turned red, and finally blurted out, "These people smile too damn much!" His anger and discomfort at the joy of others, a joy he did not have and did not want, was evident. I felt deeply for him, and I still feel deeply for others who feel as he did, for that is a very uncomfortable place to be. On the other hand, the tremendous—indeed life-changing and life-saving—changes going on in the right-end subgroups of the parish far outweighed in importance the discomfort of the left-end subgroups.

The Joe-Harry Window and Parish Levels
of Receptivity to Spiritual Rebirth

In the parish setting immediately above, there was another factor at work that gave the process of evangelism a fair chance of succeeding. Most of the subgroups in the previous section were easily discernable all the way from the Lay Pope to the Believer. The former was an authoritarian senior warden who taught local town history and reincarnation to his church school class. The latter was an elderly lady, a firm believer, who was one of the Pioneers of the parish. Because she was drawn from that strong left-end subgroup, the balance already contained a significantly different factor. I have no doubt that she prayed us into the parish.

Table 2. The Joe-Harry Window

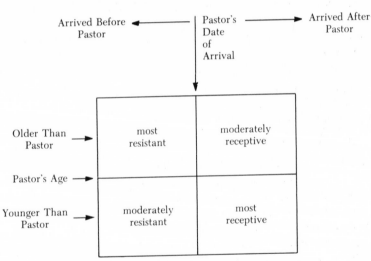

The other factor at work is reflected in the so-called Joe-Harry Window. The version of it in table 2 is an adaptation of the model provided by C. Peter Wagner in the Church Growth I course at Fuller Theological Seminary.[10] The vertical line in the center represents the date that the pastoral leader arrived in the parish. The horizontal line in the middle represents the age of the pastoral leader. Very simply, the most receptive group is the one comprised of those who are younger than the pastoral leader and have arrived in the parish after him. Least receptive is the group of those who are both older than the pastoral leader and present before he arrived. There are exceptions to this, such as Non-Status members and the Old Lonely, but the window has proven to be surprisingly accurate in my pastoral experience. In fact, generally the left-end subgroup members fall into the "most resistant" box. The right-end subgroups, while dominantly fitting into the most receptive box, are also sometimes drawn from the "moderately resistant" box, as well as from the "moderately receptive" and "most receptive" boxes. Of course, there are always exceptions to the rule, like the Believer mentioned above. These exceptions provide openings into webs of relationship within their subgroups that may provide an opportunity for careful evangelization.

Continuing pastoral care provides a significant way across the boundaries of age and time of arrival and across the boundaries of all the subgroups, although in the case of left-end subgroups the long-term effect may be governed by the strength of the subgroups and the family clusters. Win Arn has rated receptivity on a scale according to life situations. The ratings for the top fifteen, rated from 100 for most responsive down to 39 for a lower responsiveness, are given below.[11]

   100 Death of a spouse
   73 Divorce
   65 Marital separation
   63 Jail term
   63 Death of a close family member
   53 Personal injury or illness
   50 Marriage
   47 Fired from work
   45 Marital reconciliation
   45 Retirement
   44 Change in family member's health
   40 Pregnancy
   39 Sex difficulties
   39 Addition to family
   39 Business readjustment

Not mentioned above, but very significant for Episcopalians, are baptism and confirmation and the times of preparation leading up to those events. On Arn's list they should be rated with a 50, along with marriage. Only of slightly lesser importance is the entry of the oldest child into preschool or kindergarten. That event should rate at least a 45, as that change within the family often brings the young family back to the parish for church school. There is also at that time a greater sense on the part of parents that their children can be left in nursery, Sunday morning parish child care, or church school, while the parents themselves test the waters in the Sunday morning worship service. Follow-up pastoral calls from the clergy and from a parish visitation team are essential here, as this is a primary opportunity for building attendance through the incorporation of previously nominal nonparticipating members of the parish and others who are looking for a church at this significant time of their lives. On Arn's list, "change of residence" only rates 20.[12] My experience is that moving frequently places nominal Christians, who were active in other parish settings, within the Sunday morning congregation in the new community—with a very significant difference. Where they previously may have firmly belonged to any one of the left-end subgroups, by moving they have automatically joined the New People subgroup on the right end, and perhaps in the new setting they potentially could end up in the Non-Status group. This is a substantial loss of identity that often makes them very open to evangelization.

Positive and Negative Parallel Developments within the Parish

There are always two possible major responses to the proclamation of the gospel and the call to conversion. Father Donovan in *Christianity Rediscovered* records his shock at the rejection of the gospel by one of the tribes he was working with.

> Perhaps the most important lesson I was ever to learn in my missionary life, I learned that day: that Christianity, by its very essence, is a message that can be accepted—or rejected; that somewhere close to the heart of Christianity lies that terrible and mysterious possibility of rejection; that no Christianity has any meaning or value, if there is not the freedom to reject it.[13]

This is often a very difficult and painful lesson for the pastoral care giver and for other believers within the congregation who are supporting the work of the evangelization of nominal Christians in their midst. It is difficult because taking the risk to address another about the reality and joy of a possible relationship with Jesus is a love risk that often takes considerable courage. The evangelist within the parish setting may be making an objective attempt to separate the rejection of the message from personal rejection. However, human nature does not separate this well or successfully all the time. Certainly some of those who reject the message may verbally reject the bearer, but those are the risks of love. Donovan points out the dilemma presented by the nominal Christian in our midst. Speaking of the gospel he says,

> It must be presented in such a way that rejection of it remains a distinct possibility. The acceptance of it would be meaningless if rejection were not possible. It is a call, an invitation, a challenge even, that can always be refused. The Christianity of a born Catholic or of a produced Catholic (the result of an automatic baptism following a set period of instructions) which is never once left open to the freedom of rejection, to the understanding that it is a thing freely accepted or rejected—is a dead and useless thing.[14]

That element of freedom, without feelings of social coercion, must also be preserved within the context of the parish. Along with that, the love with which the gospel message is presented must be like the love Jesus describes in the Sermon on the Mount:

> You heard that it was said, "You shall love your neighbor and hate your enemy." But I say to you, Love your enemies and pray for those who persecute you, so that you may be sons of your Father who is in heaven; for he makes his sun rise on the evil and on the good, and sends rain on the just and on the unjust. For if you love those who love you, what reward have you? Do not even the tax collectors do the same? And if you salute only your brethren, what more are you doing than others? Do not even the Gentiles do the same? You, therefore, must be perfect, as your heavenly Father is perfect.[15]

The persistence of that kind of love and openness to the resistant will keep the doors open although the growing number of new converts within the congregation will demand an increasingly greater proportion of the pastor's actual time.

Hans Küng describes an important dynamic on the positive side that maintaining an open door for the freedom to choose makes possible:

> There are people, often with a religious education, who in practice never think of God for years and then discover—sometimes in very odd ways—that God could mean much, could even be decisive, not only at death, but for their life here and now. And there are people, put off or left cold by the dogmatisms and "fairy stories" of the Church's instruction, who for many years make nothing of Jesus in his mythological framework and then—again frequently in odd ways—reach the conclusion that he might mean much and even be decisive for their understanding of man, the world and God, for their existence, action and suffering.[16]

On the other hand, Küng, like Donovan, points out that

> in the last resort therefore man can say "No" to Jesus and nothing in the world can prevent him from doing this. He can find the New Testament interesting, beautiful, readable, edifying; he can call the man of Nazareth sympathetic, fascinating, moving, even a true Son of God—yet get along without him in his daily life.[17]

The presentation of the gospel is always met by those two alternating possibilities. Each individual's response to the call to conversion will be strongly affected by subgroup membership, as well as age and time of arrival in the parish in relation to that of the presenter of the message. There are other factors, all of them not entirely obvious. C.S. Lewis' character Screwtape ferrets out another, a mere habit of mind:

> The Christians describe the Enemy as one "without whom Nothing is strong." And Nothing is very strong: strong enough to steal away a man's best years not in sweet sins but in dreary flickering of the mind over it knows not what and knows not why, in gratification of curiosities so feeble that the man is only half aware of them, in drummings of fingers and kicking of heels, in whistling tunes he does not like, or in the long, dim labyrinth of reveries that have not even lust or ambition to give them a relish, but which, once chance association has started them, the creature is too weak and fuddled to shake off.[18]

Table 3 demonstrates an adaptation of the Engel Scale, which charts the spiritual decision process.[19] The Engel Scale is represented by the right-hand column. On the left hand I have placed another column charting the likely negative reactions of those who do not respond favorably to the message. The negative reactions are as predictable and graphable as the right-hand positive response, and it is a great help for those involved in the process of evangelism of nominal Christians within the congregation to understand that the unfavorable reactions fit a general pattern and are not something merely produced by the personalities of the presenters.

The right-hand column adds, after "Folding," the categories of gift development and ministry development as logical extensions of the awakening of baptism and confirmation.

Table 3. An Adaptation of the Engel Scale: Positive and Negative Parallel Developments

− 7 Exposure to empowered message	− 7 Exposure to empowered message
− 6 Grasp of implications	− 6 Grasp of implications

− 5 Denial of personal application	− 5 Abandonment of presumption
− 4 Distaste for message	− 4 Desire
− 3 Denial of personal realities	− 3 Personal problem recognition
− 2 Rejection of message	− 2 Decision to act
− 1 Antipathy to message	− 1 Repentance
0 ANGER	REGENERATION—A NEW CREATURE
+ 1 Rebellion toward message and life implications	+ 1 Postdecision evaluation
+ 2 Persecution, ie., gossip, backbiting	+ 2 Folding/teaching/witnessing identifiable disciples
+ 3 Power struggle	+ 3 Gift development
+ 4 Withdrawal	+ 4 Ministries
THE POTENTIAL IS PERMANENT ALIENATION FROM GOD.	THE POTENTIAL IS MEMBERSHIP IN THE CHURCH TRIUMPHANT NOW AND FOREVER.

The potential tragedy of the evangelism of nominal Christians within the worshiping congregation is that they may indeed say "No!" and not stop there but take an active part in opposing the presentation of the message to others. On the other hand, the potential joyous victory is that the empowered message will change the hearts and lives of many within the congregation. The outcome will be primarily dominated by the factors mentioned above: the subgroups, ages of people involved, their tenure in the parish, the availability of significant life situations to provide openings for the gospel and the accompanying pastoral care, and unknown factors represented by Screwtape's remarks on "Nothing."

The Place of Pastoral Fallibility in Relation to Evangelism

In October 1987, I was privileged to take part in a two-week mission in Ecuador with Sharing Our Ministries Abroad. The mission involved witnessing and teaching in the midst of the primary lay leaders in the Diocese of Ecuador. Due in part to the leadership of its bishop, who follows consciously the principles of Roland Allen, an Anglican missionary to China born in 1868, and due to the ongoing ministry of Sharing Our Ministries Abroad, which started a tremendous movement of the Spirit in Ecuador, there has been rapid church growth in the *Iglesia Episcopal del Ecuador:* sixty new parishes in one calendar year. Central subjects of concern were evangelism and the ministry of healing. At the personal request of the Bishop of Ecuador, the Right Reverend Adrian Caceres, I returned with my wife and two translators in June 1988. Rapid church growth has caused the Diocese of Ecuador to subdivide. The coastal plain area now forms the Diocese of Littoral, with a new bishop, the Right Reverend Luis Caisapanta. Our mission in each diocese was to teach the clergy and a small group of lay leaders who were enrolled in the training school serving both dioceses. Most of the lay leaders in this group are preparing for ordination. All of them are actively involved in founding new missions, usually more than one per person. The majority of those present in the conferences of the second mission were present in the earlier one in October 1987. In addition, in 1988 I was able, with my wife and one of the translators, to spend a week of meetings, often more than one a day, in a number of the parishes in the barrios of Guayaquil and the small towns of Los Rios.

It had been apparent to Bishop Caceres, and to me, that the clergy and lay leaders related exceptionally well to me, not only as a teacher, but as a man and a priest. One of the factors involved in this is, no doubt, that as a visiting priest from another diocese miles removed from their own I shared the common experiences of parish priests and other evangelists and at the same time I was safe in the sense that they were not accountable to me. Bishop Caceres, in taking note of this, asked me to serve as a counselor and confessor for the clergy while I was there in July 1988. My wife, Diana, served as a counselor for a number of the wives and other women involved in leadership roles during the same time. The second mission was so successful that we have been invited back for a third trip in the summer of 1989, this time for a three-week period of teaching the clergy and lay leaders of both dioceses in combined sessions on an intensive basis.

A major insight for me came with the deepening relationships with the Ecuadorian clergy and lay leaders, including that of acting as a confessor for some of them. In the midst of a very rapidly expanding church, virtually under revival conditions with frequent multiple conversions and medically verifiable healings, the clergy and lay leaders are very much like the clergy and lay leaders in the United States. Some of them are industrious; some are lazy; some are affable; some have difficult personalities; some have their lives and spirituality more or less straightened out, and others do not. There is evidently nothing in this very human group of clergy and lay leaders, each of them imperfect beings, that is a substantial block to evangelism, renewal, and the growth of the Church in Ecuador.

Granted, some were better at it than others, but the reason for that seemed not so much a matter of personal life as a varying grasp of the simplicity of the gospel and a willingness to use very simple techniques to bring people to Christ. From the viewpoint of McGavran and the application I have made of his axis of receptivity, a glaring difference in settings must be noted. The *Iglesia Episcopal del Ecuador* is growing like wildfire among the poor in the barrios and villages where they reside. They are on the right end of the axis of receptivity. By far the majority of each Ecuadorian parish is composed of Non-Status people in relationship to the crucifying structures of their society. That condition does not exist in the parishes of the United States as a general rule, and each parish needs to be evaluated on an individual basis according to its subgroups, age and tenure dynamics, and varying levels of education and sophistication in a way that hardly applies to Ecuador. Yet still within the United States, we who share with our own lay leaders the responsibility of bringing people to a personal knowledge of Jesus and his saving grace are faced with the problem of breaking through the nominalism of so many of our members. In Ecuador the problem is also nominalism. The majority of the current converts have been baptized in another denomination, in the fashion that Donovan has mentioned, without having a living faith.

The second major difference between the clergy and lay leaders in the *Iglesia Episcopal del Ecuador* and ourselves in the United States is in their handling of evangelism. They are not afraid to look someone in the eye and ask, "Have you accepted Jesus as your personal Savior?" They know enough when they hear the reply, "I hope so," to understand that the word *hope* usually means the person isn't sure. They are not afraid to explain the gospel in simple terms and to ask the person they are talking with for a decision, and they are not afraid to lead them in a simple prayer of acceptance of Jesus as Savior and Lord. They know enough to make sure the person has a Bible and begins to read it, and they know enough to involve the person in their fledgling Christian communities. Beyond that, they are involving people in discovering their spiritual gifts and actively involving them in the evangelistic ministry of establishing new parishes. They have taken the teaching of the Sharing Our Ministries Abroad missions and are actively applying them.

The message and its presentation, however, was developed here in the United States where people like myself have been working out the basic simple principles in American parishes. Because we are not on the far right end of the receptivity scale in our parishes, our experience with results does not match theirs, but the essential message is the same. The central block to nominal Christians accepting Jesus as Lord and Savior is that we often fail to simply ask them if they would like to do that. The incredible thing is that when asked, with compassion and a willingness to listen as well as to speak, so many of them, in fact, are glad to say yes. The risk lies not so much in the initial call to conversion as it does later when the dynamics of the parish begin to change because of new life and the power in the parish begins to shift from the left-end subgroups to the right end.

While the normal vagaries of the all too human lives of clergy and lay leaders do not seem to be a block to the presentation of the gospel, distinctly aberrant behavior does. Glittering sins, publicly broadcast, make the work more difficult. So does obvious immorality and occasional stubborn insensitivity. In relationship to this, the words of Craston in *Open to the Spirit* are applicable. "It has been said that God's primary concern is with his workman rather than the work."[20] I believe that as a general rule of thumb we cannot take a person any further spiritually than we have come ourselves. If we don't know Jesus ourselves in a personal way, we have little to offer as evangelists. If our lives still manifest glittering sins, these will block the spread of the gospel. If we cannot listen and will not risk love, we probably won't get a hearing. On the other hand, barring glittering sin, no matter how well or how poorly we perform, the responses to the gospel depend more on the reality of the hearer and the realistic threat of the gospel message than on the bearer of the message. Other than not obviously getting in the way, and other than making the message simple and clear, the presenter is not nearly as important as whom he presents, the message himself. A result of this observation is the knowledge that we don't have to make ourselves perfect to begin to call nominal Christians to Jesus; we simply have to take the risk and do it.

Timing is important, but timing in large part can only be learned by experience. Within the context of ongoing pastoral ministry, and within the natural context of preaching and Holy Eucharist, natural occasions arise where it is clearly appropriate to extend a general invitation, or to invite an individual, or perhaps even a family group, to accept Jesus as Lord and Savior. There are other times when it is not so clear. This is particularly true of personal invitations to strong members of left-end subgroups. Here the caution of Johnson and Malony needs to be observed:

At the point of an explicit witness, the therapist must realize that he/she does not necessarily have to bring the person to the moment of conversion. There are many links in the chain of events in a person's conversion. The therapist must be available to midwife in the process of new birth. However, as with all evangelistic endeavor, the therapist must beware of precipitating a premature birth.[21]

A driven and compulsive approach to the presentation of the gospel and the desire to bring people to Jesus only serves to deepen the possible resistance. On the other hand, asking with a clear willingness to hear and accept a no or a not yet or an "I'd like to think about it" is a legitimate part of the evangelistic process. People do need to know that there is something they can do about the gospel message, even though it may take a passage of time and a growth of courage or a deepening self-perception before they are able to say, "Yes. Now I want it!"

One of the most satisfying experiences that someone involved in evangelism can have is the experience of actually leading someone to Jesus as Lord and Savior and watching the resulting positive changes and growth in their life. The words of Paul become personalized: "For though you have countless guides in Christ, you do not have many fathers. For I became your father in Christ Jesus through the gospel. I urge you, then, be imitators of me."[22] We are not always successful. Even the best message, presented with the greatest skill and love, can be met with tremendous hostility. When an average person presents the message with clarity and all the skill and love he or she has, that hostility may be directed at the presenter in very personal ways. As Jesus said, "Woe to you, when all men speak well of you, for so their fathers did to the false prophets."[23] That experience is obviously an ancient one. The fourteenth-century mystic Henry Suso describes a vision one of his spiritual children had of him that eloquently speaks to this situation.

Once in her devotions, she went into an ecstasy, and she saw the Servant saying Mass on a high mountain. She saw an immense host of persons living in him and attached to him. But all were not in the same position: the more each had of God in him, the more they lived in the Servant also; and the more closely they were united to him, the more God had turned to them. She saw how fervently he prayed for them to the eternal God, whom he held in his priestly hands; and she asked God to explain to her what this vision meant. Thereupon God answered her thus: "The vast number of these children who cling to him are all the people who are taught by him, who listen to him, confess to him, or are devoted to him in any other way with

special affection. He drew them to me in such a way that I will bring
their lives to a good end, and see that they are never to be separated
from my joyous countenance. But whatever sufferings may befall him
as a consequence of this, he shall be well rewarded by me."[24]

Spiritual Warfare and Resistance to the Gospel

Within the ethos of the American Episcopal Church, although not
necessarily within that of the burgeoning Third World development
of the Anglican Communion, there are three levels of understanding, regarding conflict, that we are apt to approach with
increasing anxiety and distaste as we step down to each.

The first level of discomfort is reached in looking at Karl Barth's
observation of the Church in the world. At the present time within
the Episcopal Church there is strong conflict generated by whether
or not we ought to be acceptable to the world, especially in practical
ethical matters such as the issues of abortion, contemporary sexual-
ity, and the ordination of homosexuals. The issues have been bitterly
debated on both sides at the General Conventions of the church
in recent years. Stepping down to the first level of understanding
is uncomfortable for many. Barth says of the Church,

> For it claims both a very different origin and a very different goal.
> But how can the world and other human societies fail to be alienated
> if it does this seriously and effectively, if it exists within it as a living
> and growing community, and if it looks like making itself prominent
> both by the audible presentation of its universal message and if
> possible by the increase of its adherents. . . . It proclaims Jesus Christ
> and therefore a new and different humanity; the dominion of God
> over all dominions; the great freedom and necessity of conversion,
> of the *vivificatio* which inevitably involves *mortificatio;* discipleship
> and the cross. To hear this willingly and not unwillingly, or even
> thoughtfully and not with scorn and anger, to accept the Christian
> community if not seriously to receive its Word: this is not a human
> possibility. . . .[25]

It deepens our discomfort to step down to the next level and
recognize with Bonhoeffer that those who think the thoughts of the
world can create tumult in the local parish when they try to claim
the local church for their own.[26] That is also part of the message
of Barth, who says of the Church,

> But its life and growth are continually menaced. They are threatened
> both inwardly and outwardly by the world and inwardly by itself
> (in so far as it is a part of the world in its human status). The question
> is whether it will be able to overcome this danger, to be upheld in it.[27]

Our discomfort with both these descending levels of understanding must be alleviated by appealing to the psychological and sociological factors that share in the creation of these dynamics. Both the psychological and sociological facts are true and must bear their full weight in developing an adequate picture of possible conflict. But that picture is incomplete, and thus seriously flawed, unless we take the third step down to the issue that is very difficult for many of our contemporaries within the Episcopal Church to take seriously without reductionism or demythologization. One of our most popular Anglican authors, C.S. Lewis, has broached the subject in *The Screwtape Letters:*

> There are two equal and opposite errors into which our race can fall about the devils. One is to disbelieve in their existence. The other is to believe, and to feel an excessive and unhealthy interest in them. They themselves are equally pleased by both errors, and hail a materialist or a magician with the same delight.[28]

The whole premise of that popular and delightful book is that there are devils whose entire task is blocking individuals from conversion, and failing that, their task becomes that of nullifying any decisions that have already been made. Wormwood's fondly devouring uncle, Screwtape, makes this abundantly clear.

> I note with grave displeasure that your patient has become a Christian. Do not indulge the hope that you will escape the usual penalties; indeed, in your better moments, I trust you would hardly even wish to do so. In the meantime we must make the best of the situation. There is no need to despair, hundreds of these adult converts have been reclaimed after a brief sojourn in the Enemy's camp and are now with us. All the *habits* of the patient, both mental and bodily, are still in our favour.[29]

Lewis is dealing with the traditional view of temptation that always has been part of the Church's teaching. The entire purpose of temptation is to deflect humankind from the narrow way to the detriment of its salvation. As a result, any treatment of the dynamics of resistance to conversion is incomplete without taking this serious area into account. The subject of resistance to the gospel is ultimately a subject about spiritual warfare. While there are a number of contemporary sources dealing with this area, none is more insightful than the ancient spiritual classic by Athanasius, *The Life of Antony.* Conscious spiritual warfare was a subject much on Antony's mind. In this biography, Antony is recorded as saying of the demons,

> Should they see any Christians—monks, especially—laboring gladly and advancing, they first attack and tempt them, placing stumbling blocks in the way. Their stumbling blocks consist of evil thoughts. But we need not fear their suggestions, for by prayers and fasting and by faith in the Lord, they are brought down immediately. But even after they fall they do not cease, but approach again, with malice and cunning.[30]

St. Paul points out that

> . . . we are not contending against flesh and blood, but against the principalities, against the powers, against the world rulers of this present darkness, against the spiritual hosts of wickedness in the heavenly places.[31]

One conclusion to draw from the two statements above is that our conflict is not primarily with people but with negative spiritual powers who interject spiritually destructive thoughts in our minds and in the minds of those who oppose the gospel. None of us is free from this opposition. Those who actively oppose the proclamation of the gospel and the call to the conversion of nominal Christians within existing congregations are themselves victims, as all of us are. Antony warns us that

> the assault and appearance of the evil ones, on the other hand, is something troubling, with crashing and noise and shouting—the sort of disturbance one might expect from tough youths and robbers. From this come immediately terror of soul, confusion and disorder of thoughts, dejection, enmity toward ascetics, listlessness, grief, memory of relatives and fear of death; and finally there is a craving for evil, contempt for virtue, and instability of character.[32]

As for "enmity toward ascetics," one could just as easily say enmity toward consciously converted Christians or enmity toward those who proclaim an experience of personal salvation and encounter with Jesus or enmity toward any parish that dares to do so.

Antony does not artificially divide these interjected thoughts from human responsibility or from the natural bent of humankind. He is not saying that the human mind is a blank slate on which demons inscribe their evil thoughts. Far from it. The process of successful temptation finds its origin in human weakness and in our natural proclivity, hence the validity of psychological and sociological observations. The demons leap on our weaknesses and make them unmanageable apart from grace. If a person is reacting out of the fears and resistances of a particular subgroup in relation to the gospel, that reaction will be deepened by the work of the evil ones.

> For when they come, their actions correspond to the condition in which they find us; they pattern their phantasms after our thoughts. Should they find us frightened and distressed, immediately they attack like robbers, having found the place unprotected. Whatever we are turning over in our minds, this—and more—is what they do. For if they see that we are fearful and terrified, they increase even more what is dreadful in the apparitions and threats, and the suffering soul is punished with these.[33]

A second conclusion to draw from Antony's teaching is that demons make the normal fears and antipathies of men and women to the gospel worse than they need to be, and they delight to do so. Third, removing the effects of demonic interference will not completely cure the problem because the initial opening for the work of the evil ones was in the weakness of the individual in the midst of his or her subgroup. Fourth, finding ways to counter the work of the enemy will improve the situation so that the individual or group in question has a better chance to deal with fears and anxieties about the gospel. Here again the issues of freedom of will, the power of the subgroup, and age and tenure consideration must be met with patience and with whatever ongoing pastoral care people are willing to receive.

Spiritual Tools for Spiritual Warfare

Flowing directly from the propensity of the evil ones to leap on the natural fears and resistance of those who resist the gospel is the homiletical task of biblical preaching, not just an explication of the written word, but also directed to the actual fears and possible reactions of some of the subgroups in order to provide a way of reducing their fears to realistic levels. For instance, a threatened sense of loss of identity experienced by Pioneers needs to be directly addressed. But a sound homiletical and psychological principle needs to be observed. Never try to take something away without giving something better in return. The obvious gift is identity as a child of God, as an empowered member of his working Body (working means belonging), and a place in the affairs of the kingdom, not just of a parish structure.

Within the context of sermons, or at other educational opportunities, the congregation needs to be instructed carefully in the meaning of the three renunciations in the service of Holy Baptism in *The Book of Common Prayer:*

> *Question* Do you renounce Satan and all the spiritual forces of wickedness that rebel against God?

Answer   I renounce them.

Question Do you renounce the evil powers of this world which corrupt and destroy the creatures of God?

Answer   I renounce them.

Question Do you renounce all sinful desires that draw you from the love of God?

Answer   I renounce them.[34]

Along with the instruction, the members of the congregation need to be encouraged to participate anew in the renunciations as a personal act, either by joining in the responses with the parents, sponsor, and those old enough to speak for themselves or at a special time in the midst of an instruction sermon. The clearer their understanding, the more effective will be the act of renunciation. The limitation of this method is that it will only be effective for those who understand and willingly participate in the renunciation. There inevitably will be at those times some who resist sharing in this type of process because of an antipathy to the expression of these realities. Yet even with that limitation, this method will be effective for some who were borderline in their understanding of and reaction to this area.

Even though a church may have been blessed by a bishop a number of years previously, there remains a place for the use of sentences of exorcism for the restraint and banishment of evil forces. There are circumstances where the restraint of evil may be extremely helpful at the beginning of an evangelistic sermon or teaching and at times of unusual stress. A suitable prayer for this is actually provided by the Prayer Book in the service of Compline. Even though that is a service to be used on retiring in the evening, the prayer has much broader applicability. It could, for instance, be used as the prayer at the beginning of the sermon or be used silently during a difficult circumstance that you suspect is being made worse by malign spiritual forces.

> Visit this place, O Lord, and drive far from it all snares of the enemy; let your holy angels dwell with us to preserve us in peace; and let your blessing be upon us always; through Jesus Christ our Lord. *Amen.*[35]

The Bishop of Exeter in England convened a diocesan commission to investigate this whole area. The result is published in a work titled *Exorcism.*[36] The report provides forms for the exorcism and blessing of both places and people and provides clear directions for their use. A form provided for the exorcism of a place reads as follows:

*God, the Son of God, who by death destroyed death, and overcame
him who had the power of death,
  Beat down Satan quickly.*
[here he may then make the sign of the cross over the place, or exhale
deeply]
*Deliver this place (room, house, church) from all evil spirits; all vain
imaginations, projections and phantasms; and all deceits of the evil
one; and bid them harm no one but depart to the place appointed
them, there to remain for ever.*
God, Incarnate God, who came to give peace, bring peace.[37]

Even if the church has been previously blessed, it is not immune
to recurrence of the presence of demons. The report goes on to say,

> Places—churches, houses, towns, countryside—may be strained and
> influenced by a variety of causes, and frequently by more than one
> of them at a time. Among these causes may be listed: Souls of the
> departed. . . . Magicians claim to be able to instigate and operate
> "haunts." . . . Human sin: . . . sexual misbehavior . . . greed or
> domination. . . . Place memories . . . Poltergeist . . . Demonic
> interference. . . .[38]

In the general instructions on forms of exorcism, the following
instructions are given:

> (a) All forms in ordinary use should contain, in the context of either
> prayer or command, an order to the demon (i) to depart, (ii) to harm
> no one and, most importantly, (iii) to depart to its own place, there
> to remain for ever.
>
> (b) The form of exorcism may take the form either of a prayer to
> Almighty God, or of a command in the name of Christ to the powers
> of evil. It would seem that older formulae were usually addressed
> to God, but the earliest on record is the word *Exi! (Get out!)* addressed
> to a demon by a nun. . . .
>
> (c) The Lord's Prayer itself is a form of exorcism. It begins with an
> invocation of the holy name, and ends with a petition for deliverance
> from the evil one. It is very suitable for use with that intention by
> the laity, either in times of personal temptation or when in a group
> which is involved in a tense and potentially evil situation.[39]

Another obvious approach is that of intercessory prayer specifically for each member of the parish by name. A priest or pastor
can only handle that on a rotating basis, but a team of lay leaders
involved in the ministry of evangelism within the parish could cover
this need much more adequately.

The area of spiritual warfare is only one of the areas we are
concerned with in looking at the possibility of conflicts generated

by the proclamation of the gospel, but it is a significant area that we cannot afford to miss. To deal with all of these things takes a courage that flows from our relationship with Jesus Christ and with God our Father. To deal with these things constructively, and not fearfully or compulsively, is a work of the Holy Spirit. Those who seek to bring nominal Christians within the worshiping congregation to a personal faith in Jesus as their Savior and Lord need themselves to be living daily in their own baptism, the forgiveness of sins, and the power of new birth. They need also to be living in their confirmation, in the continuing discovery and use of the gifts of the Holy Spirit as they seek to minister to others in the midst of the Church.

Notes

1. Johnson and Malony, *Christian Conversion*, 78.
2. Ibid.
3. Dietrich Bonhoeffer, *Creation and Fall*, translated by John C. Fletcher. (New York: Macmillan, 1959), 11.
4. Donald A. McGavran, *Understanding Church Growth* (Grand Rapids: Eerdmans, 1970), 228.
5. Ibid., 301.
6. Luke 5:29–32, RSV.
7. McGavran, "The Shape of Class/Mass Society," in *Understanding Church Growth*, 239.
8. MacDonald, *George MacDonald: An Anthology*, 3.
9. Ibid., 4.
10. C. Peter Wagner and Carl George, "Church Growth Pastor," in *Church Growth I*, mimeographed notebook, (Pasadena: Fuller Theological Seminary, 1981), 9.1.
11. Win Arn, ed., *The Pastor's Church Growth Handbook*, (Pasadena: Church Growth Press, 1979), 144.
12. Ibid.
13. Donovan, *Christianity Rediscovered*, 108.
14. Ibid., 109.
15. Matt. 5:43–48, RSV.
16. Hans Küng, *Christian Challenge*, 257.
17. Ibid., 259.
18. C.S. Lewis, *The Screwtape Letters* (New York: Bantam Books, 1982), 36.
19. James F. Engel, "The Engel Scale," in *Church Growth II*, mimeographed notebook, C. Peter Wagner, (Pasadena: Fuller Theological Seminary, 1984).
20. Craston, "Preparing the Way," in *Open to the Spirit*, 11.
21. Johnson and Malony, *Christian Conversion*, 152.
22. 1 Cor. 4:15–16, RSV.
23. Luke 6:26, RSV.
24. Henry Suso, "The Life of the Servant," in *Late Medieval Mysticism*, Library of Christian Classics (Philadelphia: Westminster Press, 1957), 261.

25. Karl Barth, "The Growth of the Community," 285.

26. Bonhoeffer, *Creation and Fall*, 11.

27. Barth, "The Growth of the Community," 285.

28. Lewis, *Screwtape*, xiii.

29. Ibid., 4.

30. Athanasius, *Life of Antony*, 48.

31. Eph. 6:12–13, RSV.

32. Athanasius, *Life of Antony*, 58.

33. Ibid., 63.

34. *The Book of Common Prayer*, 302.

35. Ibid., 133.

36. *Exorcism: The Report of a Commission Convened by the Bishop of Exeter*, ed. Dom Robert Petitpierre (London: SPCK, 1972).

37. Ibid., 32.

38. Ibid.

39. Ibid., 20.

Conclusion

My title, *Leading Christians to Christ: Evangelizing the Church*, is based on an as yet unmentioned biblical presupposition. That presupposition is the "Great Commission" of Jesus to the Church at the time of his ascension into heaven. It is significant that Jesus first states the universality and comprehensiveness of his authority and then in the light of that issues a direct command to those who follow him.

> All authority in heaven and on earth has been given to me. Go therefore and make disciples of all nations, baptizing them in the name of the Father and of the Son and of the Holy Spirit, teaching them to observe all that I have commanded you; and lo, I am with you always, to the close of the age.[1]

That command gives to the Church its most fundamental reason for existence. The Church in its frailty, amid storms without and within, lives out the kenotic ministry of Jesus in the midst of the world. Given the stress that so often assails the Church from every quarter, it is amazing that it still grows. But that growth, that incorporation of ever-widening circles of those who are converted to Jesus and through him to the Father, is part of the very essence of the nature of the Church.

> The secret of the communion of saints is that it is capable of this expansion and engaged in it. . . . That the community as the communion of saints grows like a seed to a plant, or a sapling to a tree, or a human embryo to a child and then to a man, is the presupposition of the divine as well as the human action by which it is built. It grows—we may venture to say—in its own sovereign power and manner, and it is only as it does this that it is built and builds itself. The fact that the saints become, that they are conceived and born and live and act in the *communio* of all these *sancta* and therefore in mutual *communio*, is something which from first to last is primarily and properly a growth.[2]

The call of the Church to be Christlike in love, service, and justice in the world is not as though those things were an end in themselves. The call of the Church to be Christlike, to be all those

137

things and more, is meant to draw all humankind to the Father through Jesus. The basic and irrevocable fruitfulness of the Church is fully carried out only in evangelism.

> . . . the communion of saints shows itself to be fruitful in the mere fact that as it exists it enlarges its own circle and constituency in the world. It produces new saints by whose entry it is enlarged and increased. . . . What we are told is that it has the supreme power to extend in this way, that it does not stand therefore under serious threat of diminuition, and that as a subject which grows *per defi-nitionem* it has an astonishing capacity even for numerical increase. . . . It has propagated itself even where everything seemed to suggest that this was quite impossible.[3]

Whether or not any individual parish sees a numerical increase in its membership depends in part on the spiritual health of that membership as it now exists. A pastor in a difficult urban parish has testified,

> . . . our concentration on building up the body and letting the Holy Spirit sort us out has added more to the church in a year than I can remember in previous years. I believe evangelism will keep flowing only from a healthy body.[4]

Part of building up the Body of Christ is the evangelization of those nominal Christians within the worshiping congregation. As great as the difficulty of undertaking such a ministry is, equally great is the need for this task to be undertaken before extensive numerical growth of the parish can take place. The true growth of the kingdom does not take place only in outreach beyond the parish rolls; it takes place also within the parish, in a faithful and loving evangelism of those in our midst who have not yet accepted Jesus as Savior and Lord in a personal way.

Within the context of the Episcopal Church, pastoral leaders wrestle with a variety of subtle pressures. Not the least of these subtle pressures is the current fashionableness of "evangelism" within our denomination. The word carries very different freight for different people, but its fashionable general use points us outward where perhaps it is safer to look and less costly to attempt. In the words of Screwtape,

> we direct the fashionable outcry of each generation against those vices of which it is least in danger and fix its approval on the virtue nearest to that vice which we are trying to make endemic. The game is to have them all running about with fire extinguishers whenever there is a flood, and all crowding to that side of the boat that is gunwale

under. Thus we make it fashionable to expose the dangers of enthu-
siasm at the very moment when they are all really becoming worldly
and lukewarm; a century later, when we are really making them
Byronic and drunk with emotion, the fashionable outcry is directed
against the dangers of mere "understanding." Cruel ages are put on
their guard against Sentimentality, feckless and idle ones against
Puritanism; and whenever all men are really hastening to be slaves
or tyrants we make Liberalism the prime bogey.[5]

Looking at nominal Christians within the worshiping congregation
as the logical beginning place for evangelism may not be fashionable, may even at times place the stability of our individual parishes
and ministries in jeopardy. But until it is done, our shepherding
of the flock is incomplete and our outward evangelism is carried
on without an adequate base in the gathered congregation. Regardless of the very real risks,

> . . . perhaps in the end Baxter is right: "It is better that men should
> be disorderly saved than orderly damned, and that the Church should
> be disorderly preserved than orderly destroyed.[6]

Out of self-emptying love we need to ask all men and women the
simple question, "Have you accepted Jesus as your personal Lord
and Savior?" We need to start asking that question where we are,
within our own worshiping congregations.

Notes

1. Matt. 28:18b–20, RSV.

2. Barth, "The Growth of the Community," 260.

3. Ibid., 263.

4. Bryan Ellis, "Christians in Industrial Areas," in Watson, *I Believe in Evangelism*, 187.

5. Lewis, *Screwtape*, 74–75.

6. Gordon S. Wakefield, "Renewal in Past Ages," in *Open to the Spirit*, 149.

Bibliography

Allchin, A.M. "Walking in the Spirit: Freedom and Tradition in the Church's Life." In *Open to the Spirit*, edited by Colin Craston. Cincinnati: Forward Movement, 1987.

Anderson, Ray S. "Living in the Spirit." In *Theological Foundations for Ministry*, edited by Ray S. Anderson. Grand Rapids: Eerdmans, 1979.

――――. "A Theology for Ministry." In *Theological Foundations for Ministry*, edited by Ray S. Anderson. Grand Rapids: Eerdmans, 1979.

ARCIC II, *Salvation and the Church*. Cincinnati: Forward Movement, 1987.

――――. *Open to the Spirit*. Cincinnati: Forward Movement, 1987.

Arn, Win. *The Pastor's Church Growth Handbook*. Pasadena: Church Growth Press, 1979.

Athanasius. *The Life of Antony and the Letter to Marcellinus*. Translated by Robert C. Gregg. Classics of Western Spirituality. New York: Paulist Press, 1989.

Barth, Karl. "The Growth of the Community." In *Theological Foundations for Ministry*, edited by Ray S. Anderson. Grand Rapids: Eerdmans, 1979.

――――. "The Place of Theology." In *Theological Foundations for Ministry*, edited by Ray S. Anderson. Grand Rapids: Eerdmans, 1979.

Bede, The Venerable. *The Ecclesiastical History of the English Nation*. London: J.M. Dent, 1903.

Bennett, Dennis and Rita. *The Holy Spirit and You*. Plainfield, NJ: Logos International, 1971.

Boehme, Jacob. *The Way to Christ*. Edited by Peter Erb and Winfried Zeller. Translated by Peter Erb. The Classics of Western Spirituality. New York: Paulist Press, 1978.

Boff, Leonardo. *Church: Charism and Power*. New York: Crossroad, 1986.

Bonhoeffer, Dietrich. *Creation and Fall.* Translated by John C. Fletcher. New York: Macmillan, 1959.

———. *Christ the Center.* Translated by John Bowden. New York: Harper & Row, 1966.

The Book of Common Prayer. New York: Oxford University Press, 1979.

Brown, Colin, ed. *Dictionary of New Testament Theology.* Grand Rapids: Zondervan, 1975.

Brunner, Daniel. "Conversion: Five in the Process." In *Theology, News and Notes*, 33, no. 2. edited by Edmund Gibbs.

Caceres, Adrian. "Roland Allen and Ecuador." An interview by Andrew Kline. *Ministry Development Journal*, no. 15 (1988).

Chadwick, Henry, and Oulton, J.E.L. eds. *Alexandrian Christianity.* Library of Christian Classics. Philadelphia: Westminster Press, 1953.

Craston, Colin. "Preparing the Way: An Introduction to the Debate." In *Open to the Spirit*, edited by Colin Craston. Cincinnati: Forward Movement, 1987.

"The Didache." In *Early Christian Fathers*, edited by Cyril Richardson. Library of Christian Classics. Philadelphia: Westminster Press, 1953.

Donovan, Vincent J. *Christianity Rediscovered.* Maryknoll, NY: Orbis, 1978.

Edwards, O.C. "An Overview of Evangelism in the Church—New Testament Times to the Present." Address given at the Episcopal Conference on Evangelism in Dallas, TX, January 15–16, 1976. Mimeograph.

Eliot, T.S. "Murder in the Cathedral." In *The Complete Poems and Plays.* New York: Harcourt, Brace & World, 1962.

Engel, James F. "The Engel Scale." In *Church Growth II*, mimeographed notebook, edited by C. Peter Wagner. Pasadena: Fuller Theological Seminary, 1984.

Erikson, Erik. *Childhood and Society.* New York: W.W. Norton, 1963.

Exorcism: The Report of the Commission Convened by the Bishop of Exeter, edited by Dom Robert Petitpierre. London: SPCK, 1972.

Fourth World Conference on Faith and Order. "Christ's Ministry Through His Whole Church." In *Theological Foundations for Ministry*, edited by Ray S. Anderson. Grand Rapids: Eerdmans, 1979.

Fullam, Everett L. *Facets of the Faith*. Lincoln, VA: Chosen Books, 1982.

Gibbs, Edmund. "Conversion: A New Way of Living." In *Theology, News and Notes*, edited by Edmund Gibbs. 33, no. 2.

Gitari, Grace W. "The Contribution of Women to the Renewal of the Church." In *Open to the Spirit*, edited by Colin Craston. Cincinnati: Forward Movement, 1987.

Gore, Charles. *The Epistles of St. John*. London: John Murray, 1920.

———. *The Holy Spirit and the Church*. New York: Charles Scribners, 1924.

Green, Michael. *Evangelism in the Early Church*. Grand Rapids: Eerdmans, 1970.

Gutiérrez, Gustavo. *We Drink from Our Own Wells*. Maryknoll, NY: Orbis, 1984.

Hagner, Donald A. "Conversion: Our Calling to Reality." In *Theology, News and Notes*, edited by Edmund Gibbs. 33, no. 2. Pasadena: Fuller Theological Seminary, 1986.

Harper, Michael. *Spiritual Warfare*. Watachung, NJ: Charisma Books, 1970.

Hippolytus. *The Apostolic Tradition of Hippolytus*. Translated by B.S. Easton. Ann Arbor: Archon Books, 1962.

The Hymnal 1982. New York: The Church Hymnal Corporation, 1982.

Ignatius. "Letters." In *Early Christian Fathers*, edited by Cyril Richardson. Library of Christian Classics. Philadelphia: Westminster Press, 1953.

James, William. *The Varieties of Religious Experience*. New York: Modern Library, 1929.

Johnson, Cedrick B., and Malony, H. Newton. *Christian Conversion: Biblical and Psychological Perspectives*. Grand Rapids: Zondervan, 1982.

Kelsey, Morton. *Healing and Christianity*. New York: Harper & Row, 1973.

Küng, Hans. *The Christian Challenge*. New York: Doubleday, 1979.

———. "The Continuing Charismatic Structure." In *Theological Foundations for Ministry*, edited by Ray S. Anderson. Grand Rapids: Eerdmans, 1979.

———. *Signposts for the Future*. New York: Doubleday, 1978.

Lewis, C.S. *Screwtape Letters*. New York: Bantam Books, 1982.

Luther, Martin. "Preface to the Latin Writings." In *The Selected Writings of Martin Luther*, edited by T.G. Tappert. Philadelphia: Fortress, 1967.

———. "Sermons." In *Luther's Works*, edited by Hans Hillerbrand, vol. 52. Philadelphia: Fortress Press, 1974.

MacDonald, George. *George MacDonald: An Anthology*. Edited by C.S. Lewis. New York: Macmillan, 1947.

MacNutt, Francis. *Healing*. Notre Dame: Ave Maria, 1977.

McGavran, Donald. *Understanding Church Growth*. Grand Rapids: Eerdmans, 1970.

Marshall, Michael. "Evangelism and Witness." In *The Anglican Digest*, edited by C. Frederick Barbee. vol. 30, Early Pentecost. Hillspeak, Eureka Springs, Arkansas: SPEAK, 1988.

Neal, Emily Gardiner. *The Healing Power of Christ*. New York: Hawthorn Books, 1972.

Nock, A.D. *Conversion*. London: Oxford University Press, 1933.

Nouwen, Henri J.M. *The Wounded Healer*. Garden City: Image, 1979.

Origen. "On Prayer." In *Alexandrian Christianity*, edited by Henry Chadwick and J.E.L. Oulton. Library of Christian Classics. Philadelphia: Westminster Press, 1953.

Peck, M. Scott. *The Road Less Traveled*. New York: Touchstone, 1978.

Price, Charles P., and Weil, Louis. *Liturgy for Living*. The Church Teaching Series. New York: Seabury Press, 1979.

Rolle, Richard. "The Mending of Life." In *Late Medieval Mysticism*, edited by Ray C. Petry. Library of Christian Classics. Philadelphia: Westminster Press, 1957.

Rosen, Ruth, ed. *Jesus for Jews*. San Francisco: A Messianic Jewish Perspective, 1987.

Sarapion. *Bishop Sarapion's Prayer Book.* Edited by John Wordsworth. Hamden, CT: Archon, 1964.

Sanford, Agnes. *The Healing Light.* St. Paul, MN: Macalester Park, 1949.

"The Sayings of the Fathers." In *Western Asceticism*, edited by Owen Chadwick. Library of Christian Classics, Ichthus Edition. Philadelphia: Westminster Press, 1958.

Second Anglican—Roman Catholic International Commission. *Salvation and the Church.* Cincinnati: Forward Movement, 1987.

Spener, Philip Jacob. *Pia Desideria.* Translated by T.G. Tappert. Philadelphia: Fortress Press, 1964.

Suso, Henry. "The Life of a Servant." In *Late Medieval Mysticism*, edited by Ray C. Petry. Library of Christian Classics. Philadelphia: Westminster Press, 1957.

Taverner, Richard. "Postils on Epistles and Gospels." In *English Reformers*, edited by T.H.L. Parker. Library of Christian Classics. Philadelphia: Westminster Press, 1966.

Teilhard de Chardin, Pierre. *Sur l'Amour.* Tours: l'Imprimerie Mame à Tours, 1967.

Tertullian. "Apology." In *The Ante-Nicene Fathers*, edited by Alexander Roberts and James Donaldson. Grand Rapids: Eerdmans, 1976.

Tiebout, Harry M. "Surrender Versus Compliance in Therapy with Special Reference to Alcoholism," reprint from *Quarterly Journal of Studies on Alcohol* 14. Center City, MN: Hazeldon, n.d.

———. *The Act of Surrender in the Therapeutic Process.* New York: National Council on Alcoholism, n.d.

Van Ruysbroeck, Jan. "The Sparkling Stone." In *Late Medieval Mysticism*, edited by Ray C. Petry. Library of Christian Classics. Philadelphia: Westminster Press, 1957.

Wagner, C. Peter, and George, Carl. "Church Growth Pastor." In *Church Growth I*, mimeographed notebook. Pasadena: Fuller Theological Seminary, 1981.

Wagner, C. Peter. "The Evangelistic Challenge." In *Church Growth II*, mimeographed notebook. Pasadena: Fuller Theological Seminary, 1984.

Wakefield, Gordon S. "Renewal in Past Ages." In *Open to the Spirit*, edited by Colin Craston. Cincinnati: Forward Movement, 1987.

Watson, David. *I Believe in the Church*. Grand Rapids: Eerdmans, 1978.

———. *I Believe in Evangelism*. Grand Rapids: Eerdmans, 1987.

———. "Evangelism in the Local Church." Class lecture at Fuller Theological Seminary, Pasadena: CA, January 4–15, 1982.

Westin, H.M.D. "Renewal as Seen from Within a Traditional Catholic Spirituality." *Open to the Spirit*, edited by Colin Craston. Cincinnati: Forward Movement, 1987.

The Whole Duty of Man. London: R. Norton, 1687.

Wimber, John, with Kevin Springer. *Power Healing*. San Francisco: Harper & Row, 1987.

"The Wisdom of Jesus the Son of Sirach." In *Power Healing*. John Wimber with Kevin Springer. San Francisco: Harper & Row, 1987.

World Council of Churches. *Baptism, Eucharist and Ministry*. Faith and Order Paper no. 11. Geneva: World Council of Churches, 1982.